DARWIN'S
DEMISE

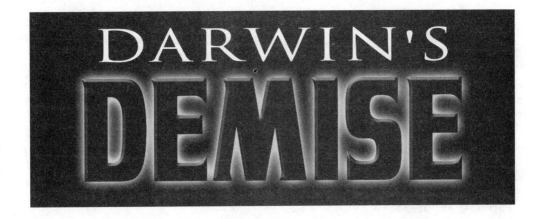

JOE WHITE, ED.D.

AND

NICHOLAS COMNINELLIS, M.D.

Master
Books

First printing: October 2001

ISBN: 0-89051-352-X
Library of Congress Catalog Number: 01-91162

Unless otherwise noted, all Scripture is from the New International Version of the Bible.

Printed in the United States of America

Please visit our website for other great titles:
www.masterbooks.net

For information regarding publicity for author interviews contact Dianna Fletcher at (870) 438-5288.

CONTENTS

CHAPTER 1

HOW DID LIFE BEGIN?

BIG QUESTIONS

1. In short, knowing the truth about our origins is essential because it affects our attitudes toward ourselves and the way we treat other people. For example, if we are indeed the end result of billions of years worth of chance biochemical reactions, as evolutionary theory tries to explain, then human nature, and even the value of human life, is quite different than if we are actually the result of an intelligent Creator who designed us.

2. The truth about our origin also has an impact on our concept of God, even our interaction with God. If humans are actually the accidental by-product of biological mutations, it's a count against there actually being any super-human power. But if we're the craftsmanship of a God who personally planned and designed humans and other creatures, then this is someone we may want to know more about.

Sorting out answers to the truth of our origins involves some fascinating work, and touches on the fields of cosmology (study of the universe), chemistry, physics, statistics, biology, genetics, paleontology, and archeology.

Finding the truth also involves a certain amount of objectivity and emotional insulation, for some people's strongest passions are kindled by this issue.

DARWIN DEFINED

For starters, let's be clear about what we mean by evolution. Prior to the mid-1800s, most people on earth believed that all living things — each type of animal, plant, and microorganism — were directly created by God, and had changed very little, if any, since that time. With few exceptions, most of the great scientists of the 17th and 18th centuries who actually invented the many disciplines that scientists practice today, believed that humans and all other creatures had been designed by a supernatural Creator.

Then in 1859 Charles Darwin published his book *Origin of Species by Means of Natural Selection,* also entitled *The Preservation of Favored Races in the Struggle for Life* or *Origin of the Species,* for short. Darwin impressed the world with the theory that all life actually began from a single cell, which over billions of years continually changed and adapted to its environment, becoming more complex and varied, and resulting today in thousands of extremely different and complex living creatures.

Darwin: A Closer Look

Charles Darwin's father and grandfather were physicians, and Charles initially sought to follow in their footsteps. In spite of being a less-than-sterling student, he entered Cambridge University in 1828, and eventually graduated with a degree in theology. After Cambridge, Darwin planned to enter the ministry somewhere in the English countryside.

One day he received a letter from Captain Fitzroy, a decorated seaman who commanded the sailing vessel *Beagle.* Darwin was offered the position of naturalist on an upcoming five-year, round-the-world ocean voyage. He accepted. During the voyage, he made copious notes of his observations, especially of the varieties within species. In particular, Darwin noticed as many as 13 varieties of finches, a small tropical bird.

Years after returning from the *Beagle* voyage, Darwin began to form his philosophy of origins. He suggested that varieties within species (such as finches) occurred spontaneously. In the struggle to survive in a harsh world, some varieties were better suited than others. Those who were superior lived and reproduced, while those who were weaker died off. He proposed that this process of spontaneous variation and "survival of the fittest" continued over billions of years, and resulted in the tremendous varieties of life we find today.

Darwin was initially praised by some as a marvelous thinker. His evolutionary approach impacted many fields, including biology, astronomy, ethics, religion, psychology, and philosophy. In stark contrast to his theological training, Darwin later demonstrated enormous contempt for anything Christian. He wrote:

The Old Testament, from its manifestly false history of the earth, was no more to be trusted than the sacred books of the Hindus, or the beliefs of any barbarian. The New Testament is a damnable doctrine. [I can] hardly see how anyone ought to wish Christianity to be true.[1]

The world rapidly accepted Darwin as an authority and adopted his explanation as fact. Within 50 years, most of the scientific community, and indeed much of the western world, had confidence in his leading. What was behind the success of his theory of evolution?

Darwin's theory of evolution today remains the most widely held explanation for the origin of life. In short, it says simply that all living things arose randomly from an inorganic, inanimate world and that certain processes led to the first original living cell. Then these same random processes caused that cell to vary and become all the varieties of creatures we observe in the world today. Single-celled creatures became jellyfish. Jellyfish became vertebrate fish. Fish became reptiles; reptiles became birds; cows became whales; apes became men.

In this theory, all living things are interrelated. Humans and apes, for example, are believed to have begun from a single animal five to twenty million years ago. Likewise, primates (which include men, horses, and apes) are believed to have begun from a single animal approximately seventy-five million years ago.

Similar connections are imagined throughout the entire animal and plant kingdoms. The study of these hypothetical relationships is called phylogeny, and they can be illustrated by a so-called phylogenetic tree.

The theory of evolution depends upon three factors. Evolutionists (people who have confidence in the theory of evolution) explain them in this way:

1. **Spontaneous generation.** This means that life arose from inanimate (dead) material. In a pond or other moist environment (referred to as the pre-biotic soup), a perfect combination of carbon-based molecules happened to be present at the same instant. Denying all scientific logic, a DNA code, nucleus, cell wall, and energy-generating apparatus — the minimum requirements for a living cell — were all somehow present, each having randomly come together on its own. This first cell reproduced itself and the first life was off to a start.

2. **Random mutation.** Minor changes in the DNA code are thought to

occur spontaneously within a creature. Most of these are attributed to "accidents" that happen when the creature's genetic code is copied at the time of reproduction. Outside radiation and chemicals are also thought to play a role.

The result of these random mutations is a new creature, slightly different from the first. Most importantly, it will either be better or less well prepared to live in its environment. Most mutations are harmful to a creature. So, a high number would be necessary to increase the chances of a positive mutation taking place.

3. **Natural selection.** Darwin realized that many more creatures were born than actually survived well. He observed a struggle for existence in which the stronger creatures survived and the weaker ones died off. This process is called natural selection.

Any random mutation that resulted in a "weaker" creature, Darwin reasoned, would cause the early elimination of that plant or animal. By contrast, any random mutation which increased the strength or fertility of a plant or animal would give it an advantage in the struggle for existence.

4. **Time.** Random mutations do not occur very often, and most mutations are damaging. Yet many positive mutations are necessary to give rise

Struggle for supremacy

to a new creature. What is needed to make the process work is time, and lots of it.

The accumulation of many small but favorable mutations over time is evolution's explanation for converting a microscopic bacterial cell into a human being. But for the process to take place requires on the order of billions of years.

TINY CHANGES DON'T COUNT

It's also important to point out what is not considered to be evolution. Evolution does not refer to changes or adaptations within a particular species of plant or animal. Rather, evolution — sometimes specified as "macroevolution" — refers to one species transforming into another. Textbooks often describe adaptations that have taken place in biology, small changes within certain species. The peppered moth of England is a frequently cited example. This process of adaptation is sometimes called "microevolution." This is an actual occurrence, a fact on which all scientists agree. A common error is made in scientific reasoning, unfortunately, when these adaptations (or microevolution) are used to assume that "macroevolution" (evolution from one species into another) also takes place.

Each species of living thing has its own unique gene pool or genetic code. Among invertebrates, protozoa, worms, snails, sponges, jellyfish, lobsters, and bees are all different basic species. Among the vertebrates, the fishes, reptiles, amphibians, and birds are clearly different species.

Consider the reptiles, which include turtles, crocodiles, and dinosaurs. Each of these is considered to be different species. Among the mammals we have bats, hedgehogs, rabbits, rats, dogs, cats, lemurs, monkeys, orangutans, chimpanzees, and gorillas, which can also be easily assigned to different species.

All humans belong to a single species, *Homo sapiens*. Tiny variations may occur within our species, such as differences in eye color, hair distribution, and skin color in the case of humans. In the case of corn, varieties seem to have arisen over the years, including starch corn, flint corn, sweet corn, pod corn, popcorn, and dent corn. Macroevolution does not refer to such limited changes; these changes do not lead to a new basic species of plant or animal.

What the theory of evolution does say is that dogs and cats arose from a common ancestor; an ancestor that over time diversified itself into mammals of different species. The theory also postulates that sparrows, finches, parrots, and black birds all came from a common forefather, such as an ancestral reptile; one who through the ages transformed itself into varieties of new species.

Some will refer to the subtle changes within a species (for example, eye color among humans) as evidence of evolution in progress, that many such tiny changes could eventually lead to a new species. The critical evidence for evolution, however, lies not in proving tiny changes, but in proving the transformation of one species into another.

BREEDING AND ARTIFICIAL SELECTION DON'T COUNT

Sometimes evolutionists point to artificial selection of plants and breeding of animals as evidence for evolution. They say that such breeding is simply evolution in fast motion, helped along by human decision-makers. Anyone with experience in grafting plants or breeding animals, however, quickly comes to three conclusions:

1. Breeding and artificial selection can accomplish only limited results. For example, an experiment was performed in France to increase the sugar content in table beets. In the beginning, the beets consisted of 6% sugar. After years of artificial selection, the sugar content increased to 17%. However, continued artificial selection did not succeed in further increasing the sugar content.[2]

2. The creature remains the same species. Even with intense breeding and artificial selection, no fundamental change occurs in the creature. Scientific experiments can create horses with shorter hair, chickens that lay more eggs, and corn with higher protein content. But in each situation, limits are reached. The breeders still ended up with the same species of horses, chickens, and corn they had in the beginning.

3. Breeding and artificial selection reduces survivability. Where modifications are made, the creature is usually weaker. It does not compete well with the original type. Falconer explains this well:

> Our domesticated animals and plants are perhaps the best demonstration of the effects of this principle. The improvements that have been made by selection in these have clearly been accompanied by a reduction of fitness, for life under natural condi-

tions, and only the fact that domesticated animals and plants do not live under natural conditions has allowed these improvements to be made.[3]

Breeding and artificial selection result in small variations only, and these are with the assistance of human genius. These are completely insufficient to prove evolution as a "natural" and spontaneous process since nothing new or complex arises, and the change accomplished is always extremely limited.

No matter what combinations may occur, the human kind always remains human, and the dog kind never ceases to be the dog kind. In fact, breeding and artificial selection may actually demonstrate the maximum limits of evolution. The most modified creatures survive only because they are kept where they have ample food, and are protected from natural enemies.

THE EVIDENCE PLEASE

To prove whether or not a theory is true requires some honest investigation. The very best evidence for the truth of a theory is to observe the subject in action. Unfortunately, it is impossible to turn back time and take notes on the early development of life on our planet.

The next best evidence would come from constructing an experiment to test whether or not evolution seems to be currently happening, or is even a possibility. However, evolution is said to only take place only over millions of years, making such an experiment impossible to undertake!

Lacking the above options, we are left with looking for indirect evidence of evolution. This evidence can come from three main sources:

• **Probability.** Spontaneous generation and random mutations are events that can be mathematically predicted. Natural selection can also be statistically analyzed. If evolution is indeed true, we should find that the mathematical probability is reasonable. In today's scientific research, most investigations demand that the odds of being correct be at least 95%. Similarly, we would expect the mathematical odds favoring evolution to be quite good.

• **Earth Age.** Since evolution demands billions of years, determining the true age of our planet is also essential. Our investigation should also confirm that the earth is extremely old, on the order of billions of years. Otherwise, there simply would not be enough time sufficient for evolution to take place. We should also discover that throughout the earth's long life, conditions were appropriate for life to flourish. The air temperature, oxygen concentration, sunlight, and so on were suitable to support living things.

 • **The Fossil Record.** The fossil layers of the earth's outer crust serve as a museum of earlier life. If evolution is indeed true, our investigation should unearth fossils that show a steady progres-

Evolution proposes that all creatures progressed from a single, original cell.

sion of life forms from, for example, guppies to sharks, finches to eagles, and apes to humans.

We would expect that the oldest and deepest layers of fossils would contain the earliest, most primitive forms of life. As we search through younger, shallower layers, we would expect to find a gradual transition of the more primitive life forms into more complex ones. We would also expect that fossils of new life forms would not appear suddenly, but would show gradual changes or transitions.

Evolutionists claim, for example, that fish evolved into amphibians. So, we can expect to find transitional forms illustrating the gradual transition of fins into feet and legs, among other changes. Since the transition from fish to amphibian would have required many millions of years (during which time many millions, even billions, of the transitional forms must have lived) fossils of many of these transitional forms should be discovered.

If reptiles turned into birds, as is claimed, then we should also expect to find fossils with gradual extending of the front feet of the reptile into the form of wings like a bird, along with the reptile's leathery skin transforming into feathers. The fossil record ought to reveal many millions of transitional, intermediate life forms. They should fill museum collections.

The fact that many people believe evolution is true is not enough to prove it. The fact that some creatures show similarities with other creatures is insufficient to prove that they evolved from one another. If evolution is accurate, it must be supported by fossils, a very old earth, and the laws of probability. We will return to these three proofs in the coming chapters.

Creative Alternative

The only other credible explanation for life is that it was intentionally designed and created. Just looking at the layout of the earth, planets, and cosmos causes some people to be convinced that a Designer must exist. Researching the intricacies of human biological life, our genetic code and internal systems persuades thinkers that it's impossible for these to have originated by chance. Examining the claims and evidence for evolution convinces many individuals that there must be a better explanation.

The Christian view is that God both intentionally planned and produced the universe and all forms of life. Many scientists, non-religious thinkers, and other organized religions also agree. Christian views about creation,

All creatures lived together.

and many other subjects, are found in the book called the Bible. Creation is primarily explained in Genesis, at the very beginning of the Bible.

For the sake of those not familiar with Genesis, a brief overview reveals God first creating the earth, followed by originating the plants, creating the sun and stars, and then the animals. God's ultimate creative accomplishment was humankind. Genesis says little about how God created the universe, except that it happened suddenly and intentionally. God's design and initiation of the universe is often called special creation.

Genesis describes God wanting to have a close friendship with Adam and Eve, the very first created people. He even walked with them in the evenings. Adam and Eve had children, and their community grew rapidly. Genesis chapter 5 describes several generations of people before a special man named Noah was born.

Trouble was growing on earth, for people were ignoring God and treating one another cruelly. God decided to obliterate life and start over again. He chose Noah to build an ark (a giant boat) and fill it with a male and female of every type of animal.

Up until this time there was a water canopy over the earth which created a "greenhouse effect" that filtered out the sun's harmful radiation and enabled all living things to live very long, productive lives in a worldwide, subtropical climate. Large reptiles (dinosaurs), fossils (such as ferns) found in icy arctic regions, and the long lives of men and women described in Genesis (i.e., Adam lived 930 years) attest to this truth. God caused the water canopy to fall, flooding the entire earth and covering even the highest mountain. But Noah, his family, and the animals were safe in the ark. After 150 days the water level began to lower and dry land appeared. Noah opened the ark and released the animals to replenish the earth with life.

As we will see later, considerable scientific and historical evidence supports the events described in Genesis.

CREATION COMPLETED

Above, we identified each unique variety of life as a species. The first two chapters of Genesis describe God's creation of each species of plants and animal. It emphasizes that each was designed to reproduce itself. The minor changes that have occurred in living things since creation have been limited to changes within particular species.

Special creation does not eliminate the possibility of varieties occurring within species. Each was created with a large enough pool of genes to give rise to all sorts of varieties within that particular species.

Humans (*Homo sapiens*) represent a species. There are about five billion humans in the world today. Except for identical twins, no two humans are exactly alike. None have the exact same gene combination. Yet we are all still distinctly human, with the distinct species name *Homo sapiens*.

The situation with dogs is similar. All dogs are variations within the single species *Canis familutris*. Whether a little Chihuahua or a German Shepherd, a beagle or a bulldog, all dogs have the same basic gene pool that makes them distinctly dogs. Humans, of course, have bred dogs to create special breeds. But they are all still dogs.

This is one of the points at which evolution and creation stand in complete opposition. Evolution holds that transformation takes place from one species into another. Creation holds that variations within species are possible, but that no transformation into new species has occurred. Instead, all species that ever existed — dinosaurs, bacteria, plants, mammals — were created at the beginning of time, and since then no new kinds have come into being. This is consistent with what the Bible says about creation being finished on the sixth day, as recorded in Genesis 2:2.

IMPRESSIVE ADHERENTS

People who believe that life was designed and created are often known as "creationists." Many Christians and believers in various religions would be known as creationists. Furthermore, numerous scientists looking at the evidence also hold the creation account as the best explanation for life. Some of the more famous "creationist scientists" include:

Biology:
Pasteur — Developed vaccinations and the science of bacteriology
Mendel — Founded the modern science of genetics

Physics:
Newton — Discovered the law of gravity; invented the reflecting telescope
Einstein — Developed the law of relativity
DaVinci — Developed the science of hydraulics

Genetics:
Mendel — Founded the modern science of genetics

Astronomy:
Copernicus — Discovered the orbit of the planets

Albert Einstein

Electronics:
Morse — Invented the telegraph

Medicine:
Lister — Developed the science of antiseptic surgery

Chemistry:
Boyle — Developed the sciences of chemistry and gas dynamics
Davy — Developed the science of thermokinetics[4]

The number of today's scientists who adhere to creation is also impressive. Rejecting the idea of particles-to-people evolution, they are more convinced by the arguments for an orderly, intentionally planned universe. Refusing the concept that life simply began by chance, they see life as telling us something about the Creator himself.

The Evidence Please

As in the case of evolution, the very best evidence for creation would come from actually being present and observing the creation of the universe in action. Lacking this, the next best evidence would come from studying creation in action today, proving that it is scientifically possible. Scientists continue to carefully study life. However, in recorded history no new life forms (new species) have been discovered. The Genesis account, furthermore, says that creation of life forms was completed back at the beginning of time.

Without evidence like that just described, we are left with looking for indirect signs of creation. Parallel to evolution, we can look at evidence from the same three main sources:

- **Probability.** Since life is so unique and complex, we should find that the mathematical probability of it occurring spontaneously is very, very low.
- **Earth Age.** The age of the earth described in the Bible is essentially very young; on the order of 6,000–10,000 years. Since all life was created simultaneously, a longer time frame is unnecessary to explain its existence. Our scientific findings regarding earth's age should show a young planet.
- **The Fossil Record.** If creation is true, we'd expect to find a sudden, explosive appearance in the fossil record of highly complex forms of life. We would predict that fossils of all of the major types of plants and animals would appear abruptly. We also expect to find no sign of transitional forms linking one basic species to another in the fossil record.

We would anticipate finding fossilized remains of mice, lizards, cats, dogs, cows, elephants, horses, bats, dinosaurs, sharks, monkeys, apes, and men. Each species from its earliest fossils would be fully developed and possess the characteristics that set it apart from all others.

Either creation is true or evolution is true. No other possible explanation for life exists. The fact that some people believe in creation or evolution is not enough to prove that one or the other is correct. The evidence from fossils, the age of the earth, and the laws of probability must also be considered.

WATCH YOUR BIAS

Searching out honest answers to big questions is admirable. It's also difficult. One of the major obstacles comes from each person's bias. Bias means our tendency to find what we first decided we want to find, rather than what's actually there. It means our inclination to see what we really desire to see, rather than seeing what actually exists.

People are prone to let their individual bias get in the way of logical thinking. We tend to wrongly believe, for example, that whites make for better students, and blacks for better athletes. We unjustly hold that men should be doctors and women should be nurses. We undeservingly view young people as less trustworthy than those who have gray hair. Bias keeps us from living our lives consistent with the actual truth. It causes you and me to become shortsighted and to miss opportunities.

Investigating ideas of creation and evolution tends to magnify people's bias even more sharply. Some individuals don't want to be confronted with a truth that may force them to rethink their entire perspective on God, history, science, and the value of human life. It seems easier to just dig in their heels, hanging on to ideas that have little support, rather than to look at the facts and reconsider.

But denying reality has its costs. Gravity will make you fall, even if you don't believe it exists. Electricity can shock you, even though you can't see it. Grasping untrue ideas about origins can cause you to totally miss some of the most remarkable aspects of life.

It is possible for each person to overcome the power of individual bias regarding creation and evolution. Take these steps:

- Start by clarifying in your mind what it is you believe about this subject. From whom did you get these ideas? What questions do you have about them today?
- Decide in advance that you'll reconsider the evidence, and not let your previous ideas get in the way.

- Promise yourself that, if necessary, you'll change your views and try to live consistently with the truth surrounding this subject.

An hallucination consists of imagining things that don't really exist. No one honestly wants to have hallucinations. Neither do we want to fill our lives with unreal ideas. Let's find out the truth about creation and evolution.

Summing Up

How did life begin? It's not an abstract question, for the truth about our origins affects both our attitudes toward people and also our interaction with the supernatural.

The popular answer is evolution, that humans and all other living things are the result of spontaneous generation, random mutations, natural selection, and billions of years worth of time. Popular as this idea may be, evolution (if evolution is indeed true) must stand up to several tests: the probability must be reasonable, the inhabitable earth must be very old, and fossils must be found showing the transition from one new species into another.

The only other possible explanation for life is creation; that God intentionally designed and produced all living things. For evidence we'd expect to find creatures so intricate they could not have arisen on their own, a young planet consistent with the Bible's account of creation, and absolutely no fossils that show transition between creatures.

The subject of evolution and creation is complicated by people's tendency to see what they want to see, rather than seeing the facts as they really are. By keeping our bias under control, however, we can discover the real truth about how life began.

Endnotes

1 Charles Darwin, *The Origin of Species* (London: A.L. Burt, 1859).

2 M. Burton and R. Burton, editors, *The International Wildlife Encyclopedia* (New York, NY: Marshal Cavendish Corp., 1970), p. 2706.

3 W.J. Tinkle, *Heredity* (Grand Rapids, MI: Zondervan Publishing House, 1970), p. 84, quoting D.S. Falconer, *Introduction to Quantitative Genetics* (New York, NY: Ronald Press Co., 1960), p. 331.

4 A. Lamont, *21 Great Scientists Who Believed the Bible* (Australia: Creation Science Foundation, 1995, p. 120-131. Henry M. Morris, *Men of Science, Men of God* (Green Forest, AR: Master Books, 1982).

CHAPTER 2

IMPOSSIBLE ODDS!

DNA, What Do You Say?

Evolution makes some remarkable claims about how humans and other creatures came into being. The better we appreciate the unique complexity of living things, the better we can also appreciate the likelihood of life beginning by chance alone.

Even the simplest life requires enormous intricacy of structures and functions. Scientists refer to life as being characterized by incredibly specified complexity. Leslie Orgel, a well-known origin-of-life researcher emphasized this fact, saying:

> Living things are distinguished by their specified complexity. Crystals such as granite fail to qualify as living because they lack complexity; mixtures of random polymers fail to qualify because they lack specificity.[1]

Blood, the brain, the eye, the pumping heart, and the pituitary gland are fantastically elaborate organs. Some aspects of their functions are still only beginning to be uncovered, even after decades of research. Yet within each cell of these organs lie structures even more fantastic than the organ itself: deoxyribonucleic acid, or DNA.

DNA is the genetic material that carries all the instructions for the function of the cell. There are four different subunits within DNA, called nucleotides. The particular sequence of these subunits in the DNA chain is what distinguishes one gene from another.

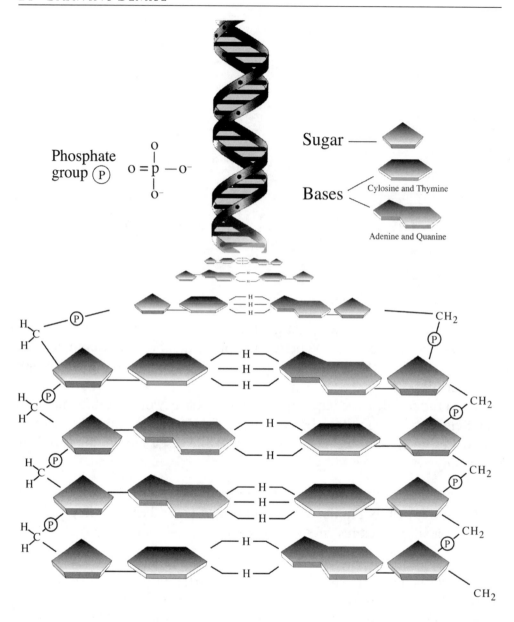

Phosphate group P

$$O = \overset{\overset{\displaystyle O}{\|}}{\underset{\underset{\displaystyle O^-}{|}}{P}} - O^-$$

Sugar

Bases

Cylosine and Thymine

Adenine and Quanine

Scientists have discovered that DNA is organized into three main levels. The "lowest" level of DNA is called base pairs. Several hundred to several thousand base pairs are then organized into genes. Hundreds of thousands of genes are present in every cell of higher animals. Large groups of genes are organized into chromosomes.

DNA determines what structures a cell will build, what chemicals or hormones it will produce, and where the cell will locate itself in the body. DNA directs the burning of energy, disposal of waste products, and reproduction of the cell. In short, it is a vast amount of biochemical information. The evolutionist Dawkins substantially underestimates the complexity of the genetic code when he writes:

> There is enough information capacity in a single human cell to store the Encyclopedia Britannica, all 30 volumes of it, three or four times over.[2]

> Not only is the amount of information in cellular DNA staggering, it's also incredibly compact. We marvel at computer storage disks with ever greater capacity. Yet the quantity of information that could be stored in a pinhead's volume of DNA is equivalent to the content of a pile of paperback books spanning the distance from earth to the moon 500 times — each book being unique from the others![3]

Since DNA contains the information needed to make the chemicals and structures of life, we'd expect the most similar creatures to have the most similar DNA. This is, in fact, the case. Apes and humans have numerous physical similarities, and have somewhat similar DNA. The DNA of scorpions is more different from that of humans, but still contains some resemblance. The DNA of bacteria is only slightly similar.

Evolutionists insist that these similarities indicate that living things evolved from one another. But there exists some other findings that are even further beyond evolution's ability to explain: resemblancs between creatures that evolutionists say evolved separately. For example:

> Hemoglobin, the molecule that carries oxygen in blood, is found in all vertebrates, including humans. But hemoglobin also exists in earthworms, crustaceans, starfish, and even in some microorganisms. . . .
> Crocodile hemoglobin is more similar to chicken hemoglobin than that of snakes and other reptiles. . . .
> Human lysozyme, an enzyme for digesting food, is more similar to chicken lysozyme than to the lysozyme of any other mammal.[4]

An identical particular protein is found on the cell wall of both camels and nurse sharks. Yet, speaking in terms of evolution, these animals are completely unrelated.[5]

These chemical similarities cannot be explained through evolutionary connections, for the creatures involved are not at all related. Similarities in DNA and other cellular chemicals do not necessarily mean that one creature evolved from another. Instead, one can reasonably argue that the similarities indicate a common designer.

WITHOUT EVERYTHING, YOU HAVE NOTHING

DNA doesn't just contain an enormous amount of information, but almost all of it must also be present for a cell to function. Consider some comparisons: A beautiful new car (weighing 2,500 pounds) can be rendered immobile if only a couple of spark plugs (weighing 4 ounces) are missing. A sleek, graceful airplane can be grounded by the removal of only one wing flap.

The minimal number of components necessary for a machine to function is called its *irreducible complexity*. Biochemist Michael Behe explains that in the mechanical world, if one essential component (such as a spark plug or wing flap) is missing, the entire machine won't operate.[6]

At the cellular level, irreducible complexity is critically important. Remove the cell membrane and the cell collapses. Separate the mitochondria and the cell has no energy. Displace the nucleus and most chemical functions of the cell cease immediately.

Similarly, the functions of many organs also show irreducible complexity. All of their components must be present and operating for the organ to fulfill its role. A small number of abnormally dark cells on the cornea will make the entire system of vision inoperative. A few atypical fibers on the heart's electrical conduction system will cause it to pump irregularly or not at all. A tiny clot of blood in a vessel of the brain will cause immediate paralysis of an arm or leg, or even death. A tiny anomalous growth on the bone touching the ear drum will render the person deaf in that ear.

NO "SIMPLE" CELLS

Living things require an enormous quantity of information, functioning in concert together. Yet many people don't grasp just how fantastic is even one "simple" cell. The simplest organism contains encyclopedic quantities of complex information. *Mycoplasma genitalium* is a bacteria with

Parts of a Typical Cell

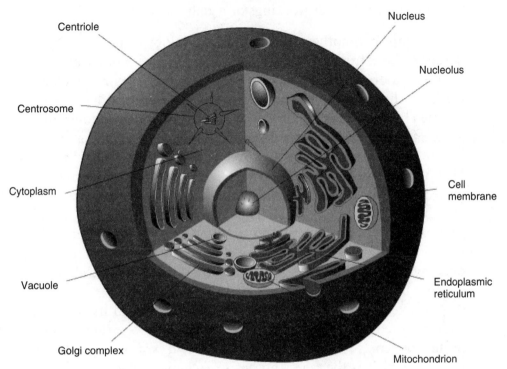

the smallest amount of genetic material of any known organism. Yet even this microscopic organism has 580,000 base pairs on its 482 genes.[7]

Even with this vast quantity of biogenetic information, *Mycoplasma genitalium* can only survive by parasitizing other more complex organisms, which provide for it nutrients, a cell membrane, and DNA replication — all of which are things *Mycoplasma genitalium* can't do for itself.

What is the bare minimum amount of genetic code necessary for a cell to "live"? Recently, Eugene Koonin and others attempted this calculation and came up with 256 genes. But they expressed doubt that their hypothetical cell could survive in reality. It would have no means to repair DNA damage or digest complex compounds, and would need to live in a near "perfect" environment.[8]

Molecular biologist Michael Denton, a critic of Darwinian evolution, gives us an idea of the inner workings of a cell:

> Perhaps in no other area of modern biology is the challenge posed by the extreme complexity and ingenuity of biological adaptations more apparent than in the fascinating new molecular world of the cell. . . . To grasp the reality of life as it has been revealed by molecular biology, we must magnify a cell a thousand million times until it is twenty kilometers in diameter and resembles a giant airship large enough to cover a great city like London or New York. What we would then see would be an object of unparalleled complexity and adaptive design. On the surface of the cell we would see millions of openings, like the portholes of a vast space ship, opening and closing to allow a continual stream of materials to flow in and out. If we were to enter one of these openings we would find ourselves in a world of supreme technology and bewildering complexity.
>
> Is it really credible that random processes could have constructed a reality, the smallest element of which — a functional protein or gene — is complex beyond our own creative capacities, a reality which is the very antithesis of chance, which excels in every sense anything produced by the intelligence of man? Alongside the level of ingenuity and complexity exhibited by the molecular machinery of life, even our most advanced artifacts appear clumsy. . . .
>
> It would be an illusion to think that what we are aware of at present is any more than a fraction of the full extent of biological design. In practically every field of fundamental biological research, ever-increasing levels of design and complexity are being revealed at an ever-accelerating rate.[9]

Great advances in biotechnology have taken place in recent years. Do these breakthroughs make the cell or living things seem more "ordinary" than before? Just the opposite is true. *Mycoplasma genitalium* is complex enough with 580,000 base pairs, yet humans have 3 billion base pairs on their genes. The DNA of a human stores enough information code to fill 1,000 books each with 500 pages of very small print (3 billion letters long). The DNA of even a single microscopic human cell is composed of 3 million units, and contains all of the information necessary to construct an entire adult human. With each advance in understanding, such as these, scientists only broaden their appreciation for the enormous intricacies of life.

Uniquely Human

The study of single-cell organisms is challenging enough to keep researchers busy for a lifetime. Multiply this effort times one trillion and we can just begin to understand the complex challenges of understanding human life. Consider some of the facts:

Cells

The human body has 100 trillion cells.

All the cells in the human body lined up side-by-side would encircle the earth 200 times.[10]

The DNA from one human cell contains a billion biochemical steps.

If all DNA in a human were placed end to end, it would reach the sun and back 400 times.[11]

A single cell contains enough information to fill 10 million books.[12]

The Eye

The human eye can handle 1.5 million simultaneous messages.[13]

In a day, the eye moves 100,000 times. (The body would have to walk 50 miles to exercise the leg muscles at an equal amount.)

137 million nerve endings within each eye pick up every visual message the eye sends to the brain.[14]

The Ear

A single inner ear contains as many circuits as the telephone system of a large city.[15]

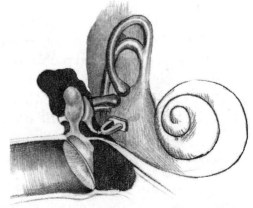

The ear is an extremely complex structure.

THE HEART

The human heart beats 40,000,000 times a year.

In a lifetime, the heart will pump 600,000 metric tons of blood.[16]

All veins, arteries and capillaries lined end-to-end would extend 80,000 miles.

A single drop of blood can be delivered anywhere in the body within 20 seconds.[17]

THE BRAIN

The information in the brain equals that contained in 20 million separate books.[18]

A machine matching the human brain in memory capacity alone would consume electrical energy at the rate of one billion watts (half of the output of the Grand Coulee Dam). It would cost $10 billion to build and fill the Empire State Building.[19]

The brain has 10,000,000,000 circuits and a memory of 1,000,000,000,000,000,000,000 bits.[20]

The human body is awesome in its complexity and resilience. Often, we take for granted our ability to see with our eyes, hear with our ears, and enjoy our other senses. An occasional illness is often a timely reminder of just how well the body does function. Of all our human abilities, one of the most amazing is language — our ability to express thoughts and feeling, and communicate this with others. Duane T. Gish expresses it well:

Of all creatures on earth, only man has the ability to use language. Not only does man have the ability to remember the past, to cope with complicated problems in the present, and to plan for the future, but he has the ability to express all of these thoughts both verbally and in written form. The human brain, with its twelve billion brain cells and 120 trillion connections, is the most complex arrangement of matter in the universe. Thus endowed, man's ability to express himself verbally and in written form is truly incredible.[21]

Life is enormously complex. The function of even the smallest cells is intricate, let alone the function of the human body. Not only is life complex, but it is complex out of necessity. Life is not possible without these complex systems.

Spontaneous Generation — The Origin of Life?

Evolution depends upon natural selection and other processes we'll discuss in a moment. A fact rarely mentioned by evolutionists, however, is that for evolution to ever get started, there first must be a very highly complex, intact, living, self-reproducing creature. And this requires spontaneous generation.

Spontaneous generation is the theory that the first life arose impromptu from the random chemicals that happened to be present. All of the minimum (and incredibly complex) cellular structures that were needed just happened to be in the same place at the same time. This pool of lifeless chemicals gave rise to a very simple amoeba-like cell. Life was off and running.

The Encyclopedia Britannica explains it like this:

> Whether the earth cooled from a molten mass or condensed out of cold dust, life could not have existed when the earth was formed some 5,000,000,000 years ago; it must have originated since. As both processes (automatic synthesis and ultraviolet light energy) are the characteristic of life, it is not unreasonable to suppose that life originated in a watery "soup" of prebiological organic compounds and that living organisms arose later by surrounding quantities of these compounds by membranes that made them into "cells." This is usually considered the starting point of organic ("Darwinian") evolution.[22]

Sound like a reasonable idea? Perhaps, until we appreciate this fact: for even the simplest cell to ever get started requires an awesomely complex assembly of chemical structures. That this could have happened through random chance is stastically impossible.[23]

DNA — containing the code for this first living cell — is very complex and does not naturally occur. In fact, the chance of you being able to jump high enough to reach the moon is greater than the chance that DNA would form at random. Its existence can only be reasonably explained by some external, organizing force.

The "simplest" one-celled organism known to man has more exactly programmed data stored within it than all of the letters in all of the books in the largest library in the world! It is impossible that an encyclopedia could have occurred at random, without intelligent design behind it. Similarly, it's just as impossible that life could have begun without intelligent design.

Louis Pasteur proved experimentally over a century ago that non-life cannot produce life, that dead objects cannot produce living ones, that each organism requires parents, and that only parents produce the new life. It has been universally held, since Pasteur, that life always arises from life of the same kind. This is the law of biogenesis. The vast majority of the world's most respected and honored scientists agree with this law. Many of these totally reject the theory of spontaneous generation. Others continue to grapple with their own inconsistencies.

Louis Pasteur

Spontaneous generation is said to have been a random, chance event, with no outside, purposeful influence. Let's examine what "chance" looks like. If you flip a coin, the probability of heads is one in two. Rolling a six on a die has the probability of one in six. Rolling nine straight sixes would be one chance in ten million. Who would bet $100 that you could roll 50 straight sixes (probability of 1 in 10^{39}) or flip a hundred straight "heads" on a coin (probability of 1 in 10^{30})?

British astronomer Sir Fred Hoyle calculated the probability of spontaneous generation:

> The likelihood of the formation of life from inanimate matter is 1 to a number with 40,000 noughts after it ($10^{40,000}$). . . . It is big enough to bury Darwin and the whole theory of evolution. There was no primeval soup, neither on this planet nor any other, and if the beginnings of life were not random, they must therefore have been the product of purposeful intelligence.[24]

Sir Fred Hoyle further explains his position, using the example of a Rubik's cube:

At all events, anyone, even a nodding acquaintance with the Rubik's cube will concede the near impossibility of a solution being obtained by a blind person moving the cubic faces at random. Now imagine 10^{50} (that's a number 1 with 50 zeros after it) blind people, each with a scrambled Rubik's cube, and try to conceive of the chance of them all simultaneously arriving at the solved form. You then have the chance of arriving by random shuffling at just one of the many biopolymers on which life depends. The notion that not only biopolymers but the operating program of a living cell could be arrived at by chance in a primordial organic soup here on the earth is evidently nonsense of a high order.[25]

Sir Hoyle vividly illustrates the probability of spontaneous generation like this:

Supposing the first cell originated by chance is like believing a tornado could sweep through a junkyard filled with airplane parts and form a Boeing 747.[26]

Professor Harold Morowitz puts the chance of spontaneous generation as being much less than even that of Sir Hoyle:

The probability for the chance of formation of the smallest, simplest form of living organism known is 1 to $10^{340,000,000}$.
This number is 1 to 10 to the 340 millionth power! The size of this figure is truly staggering, since there are only supposed to be approximately 10^{80} electrons in the whole universe![27]

To further illustrate, this is approximately the same ridiculous probability that an entire high school gym filled with dice could instantly explode and every one of the die would land on the number one!

The most renowned atheist in the latter 20th century, Dr. Carl Sagan, estimated that the mathematical probability of the simplest form of life emerging from non-living matter has the unbelievable odds of one chance in ten to the two billionth power (a 1 followed by two billion zeros after it) — even less probability than predicted by Sir Hoyle or Dr. Morowitz. The enormity of this figure is revealed by the fact that it would take 6,000 books of 300 pages each just to write the number![28]

Just how likely is an event like this? Dr. Emile Borel, who discovered the laws of probability, says:

The occurrence of any event where the chances are beyond one in ten followed by 50 zeros is an event which we can state with certainty will never happen, no matter how much time is allotted and no matter how many conceivable opportunities could exist for the event to take place.[29]

Dr. Emile Borel explains, in essence, that anything with a chance of more than 1 in 10^{50} would never happen, no matter how much time there is. So how could an event with a probability of 1 in 10 to the two billionth power ever happen? It is absolutely, empathetically impossible!

Distinguished chemist and physicist Dr. John Grebe explains how remote is the possibility that functional DNA itself — let alone a functioning cell — could randomly come together on its own:

The 15,000 or more atoms of the individual sub-assemblies of a single DNA molecule, if left to chance as required by the evolutionary theory, would go together in any of 10^{87} (1 in 10 to the 87th power) different ways.[30]

In other words, there are trillions times trillions times trillions of different ways that a single gene could have come together. Yet only *one* way would lead to a functional DNA molecule.

Evolutionists claim the universe is about five or ten billion years old. There are less than 10^{17} seconds in 20 billion years. Therefore, even if a trial and error combination occurred every second from the beginning of time until today, the odds still appear hopelessly high against the natural assembly of even this single molecule.

Take 10^{70} combinations:

10,000,000,000,000,000,000,000,000,000,000,000,000,000,000,000, 000,000,000,000,000,000,000 minus 100,000,000,000,000,000 seconds that a single DNA molecule could be formed by mere chance, and the remaining "odds" are 1 in 9,999,999,999,999,999,999,999,999,999,999,999,999, 999,999,999,999,900,000,000,000,000,000.

This means that the odds of a single functional DNA molecule coming together at random are about the same odds that you could fill a billion universes with golf balls and put a small red dot on the bottom of one ball and somehow a blindfolded baby could find that ball while rummaging through the hundred billion galaxies on the very first try.

Pierre-Paul Grassé of the University of Paris and past-president of the French Academy of Science, echoes this view:

> To insist, even with Olympian assurance, that life appeared quite by chance and evolved in this fashion, is an unfounded supposition which I believe to be wrong and not in accordance with the facts.[31]

Dr. Wilder Smith, a chemist and former evolutionist, concludes:

> It is emphatically the case that life could not arise spontaneously in a primeval soup from its kind.[32]

And Dr. Wilder Smith goes on to say,

> Furthermore, no geological evidence indicates an organic soup ever existed on this planet. We may therefore with fairness call this scenario "the myth of the pre-biotic soup."[33]

Michael Denton, Ph.D., a noted scientific philosopher, agrees:

> Considering the way the pre-biotic soup is referred to in so many discussions of the origin of life as an already established reality, it comes as something of a shock to realize that there is absolutely no positive evidence for its existence.[34]

Dr. Denton goes on to say,

> The complexity of the simplest known type of cell is so great that it is impossible to accept that such an object could have been thrown together by some kind of freakish, vastly improbable event. Such an occurrence would be indistinguishable from a miracle.[35]

Nobel Prize winner Ilya Prigogine likewise declared:

> The idea of spontaneous generation of life in its present form is therefore highly improbable even on the scale of the billions of years during which prebiotic evolution occurred.[36]

> According to Monod, another Nobel Prize winner and biochemist at the University of Paris, the possibility of life arising spontaneously "was virtually zero."[37]

Edward P. Tryon, Professor of Physics at City University of New York, reminds us of a fact that we all learned as children:

> The novelty of a scientific theory of *creation ex nihilo* (Latin for "creation from nothing") is readily apparent, for science has long taught us that one cannot make something from nothing.[38]

There is truth in the concept that nothing produces nothing. Non-life produces only non-life; zero times zero is zero even if you give it a billion trillion years.

Most of us have come across small collections of rust on the ground. What do you suppose is the possibility this rust would clump together, transform itself, and become a clean, fully functioning car, all by random chance? Impossible! And yet even the simplest living cell is vastly more complex than a car.

Spontaneous generation — the chance origin of life from dead material — is likewise scientifically indefensible. A chorus of respected scientists lifts its voice in agreement. Yet in spite of these impossible odds and voices of dissent, an influential group of teachers and textbook publishers cling to the belief that somehow it happened anyway.

"Accidents" We Can Live Without

The theory of evolution goes on to say that once the first living cell got started, two things happened that made the organism become progressively more complex. They are called the "mechanism of evolution." These are:

Random mutation. Errors in the cell's DNA, outside radiation, and outside chemicals are said to cause minor changes in the creature. Most of these are attributed to "accidents" that happen when its own genetic code is copied at the time of reproduction. The result of these random mutations is a new creature, slightly different from the first.

Natural selection. This new, slightly different creature will either be better or less well prepared to live in its environment. Any random mutation that resulted in a "weaker" creature would cause the early elimination of that plant or animal. By contrast, any random mutation which increased the strength or fertility of a plant or animal would give this "superior" creature an advantage in the struggle for existence. It would then reproduce and continue this "strain" of superior creatures.

What is the evidence to support these ideas? Does the scientific proof either demonstrate or detonate Darwin's "greatest general principle in biology"? At the time Darwin formulated the theory of evolution relatively little was known about biogenetics. Today we have the advantage of enormous information that was not available during Darwin's era. We know, for example, that genes are ordinarily very stable. Genes are almost invariably passed on from generation to generation without any alteration in structure whatsoever.

Very rarely, however, the chemical structure of a gene does undergo a change. Such a change is called a mutation. Mutations may be caused by ultraviolet light, cosmic rays, x-rays, and chemicals, as well as copying errors during reproduction. Most mutations result in one change amid the several thousand subunits within a particular gene. The DNA change itself usually is so subtle that it cannot be identified using current technology.

However, the effect of the tiny mutation on the plant or animal may be drastic. Almost all mutations are harmful to the creature, and very often prove lethal. Scientists have analyzed nature for signs of mutations, and created many in the laboratory. Of all the mutations that have been analyzed, it is doubtful that a single one can be clearly said to have increased the survivability of the plant or animal.[39]

Evolutionists assert, however, that a very small number of these mutations may be beneficial; perhaps one in 10,000. This perspective is not based on any evidence of favorable mutations. So why do evolutionists make the claim? The only reasonable explanation is that they know evolution must be ascribed to mutations, and that evolution is impossible unless favorable mutations do occur.[40]

MUTATIONS — RARE AND HARMFUL

Mutations make creatures weaker, not stronger.

Since almost all mutations are harmful to a creature, a very high number would be necessary to increase the chances of a positive mutation taking place. These hypothetical beneficial mutations are supposed to alter the plant or animal, increasing its ability to survive and/or reproduce. Evolutionists, with very few exceptions, believe that these proposed favorable mutations must result in only slight changes. A mutation that would result in more than a slight change would be too disruptive, and certainly harmful or lethal to the plant or animal.

After many thousands of generations, the "superior mutant" that developed would eventually replace the original variety of creature — a process called natural selection.

If only one out of ten thousand mutations leads to a "better" creature, the occurrence of a favorable mutation is extraordinarily rare indeed. What's more, in order for the mutation to be passed on, it cannot occur just anywhere in the creature; it must occur in the genes of the specific reproductive cells, and these make up only a minute fraction of most creatures' cells.

Research has uncovered the fact that cells have many special safeguards to protect against genetic errors ever occurring. DNA information cannot be copied except with many different enzymes, which "check" one another for errors. These include double-sieve enzymes to make sure the right amino acid is linked to the right tRNA. One sieve rejects amino acids too large, while the other rejects those too small.[41]

Scientists are convinced that the cells system of checks and safeguards is the best possible for protecting against DNA errors.[42]

Evolution, in spite of these safeguards against DNA mutation, obviously would require a vast amount of time to take place. Evolutionists claim that to slightly change one species into a new species requires many thousands of these hypothetical favorable mutations, and at least hundreds of thousands, if not millions, of years. Greater changes, such as transforming a reptile into a bird, would require an extremely large number of beneficial mutations, and demand trillions of years.

Occasionally, scientists observe minor changes within a species, called adaptation. Some moths, bacteria, and fruit flies have adapted to their environment with positive genetic modifications. But the species themselves did not change. As we discussed in chapter 1, the adaptive fruit fly remained a fruit fly; the adaptive peppered moth remained a peppered moth. No laboratory proof or paleontological proof exists that these species evolved up the scale of complexity into a more complex life form. There is no evidence of evolution from one species into another.

MUTATIONS — "NEW INFORMATION" MACHINES?

Assume, for the sake of argument, that the first cell did come into existence on its own. To travel up the evolutionary ladder from this simple beginning to a complete human being requires the cell to generate enormous quantities of new genetic information. New DNA code is essential to manufacture skin, eyes, nerves, bones, hearing, muscles, blood cells, and so forth.

However, the study of modern genetics shows that mutations lead to a net loss of information, not any overall gain. Biophysicist Dr. Lee Spetner of Johns Hopkins University states in one of his books:

> In this chapter I'll bring several examples of evolution [i.e., instances alleged to be examples of evolution], particularly mutations, and show that information is not increased. . . . But in all the reading I've done in the life sciences literature, I've never found a mutation that added information.
>
> All point mutations that have been studied on the molecular level turn out to reduce the genetic information and not to increase it.
>
> The NDT [neo-Darwinian theory] is supposed to explain how the information of life has been built up by evolution. The essential biological difference between a human and a bacterium is in the information they contain. All other biological differences follow from that. The human genome has much more information than does the bacterial genome. Information cannot be built up by mutations that lose it. A business can't make money by losing it a little at a time.[43]

Research shows that mutations, when they do occur, do not increase the total amount of information contained by a cell. Rather, they decrease it. So how can mutations possibly account for the enormous amount of new information required by advanced creatures?

To further illustrate the challenge of "creating" new genetic information, consider this: Sometimes evolutionists point out that the similarity between DNA of various creatures shows they must have transformed from one into the other. The similarity between human and ape DNA, for example, is said to be 96 percent by one limited technique. But the cells of every creature contain enormous quantities of information content, so even a small percentage difference means that tremendous quantities of information would be required to turn one kind into another. Since humans have an amount of information equivalent to one thousand 500-page books, a 4 percent difference amounts to 40 large books of information.

Now, evolution says that random mutation plus natural selection generated the information equivalent to these 40 large books — 12 million words arranged in intelligible sentences. Creating this amount of new genetic code is impossible, even if we give it the ten million years that evolutionists say were required for apes to evolve into humans!

Population genetics calculations show that animals with 20 years between each generation could pass on no more than about 1,700 mutations in these ten million years.[44]

But only perhaps one mutation in 10,000 is beneficial. So how could mutation and natural selection ever achieve all the millions of beneficial mutations needed to transform apes into humans? It would require trillions upon trillions of years!

By the sixth edition of his own book, Darwin himself abandoned his own theory. He wrote: "Natural selection is incompetent to account for the incipient stages of useful structures."

Modern scientists wholeheartedly agree. Radiation and mutation expert Dr. H. J. Muller, in the publication *Bulletin of the Atomic Scientists* writes:

> It is entirely in line with the accidental nature of mutations that extensive tests have agreed in showing the vast majority of them detrimental to the organism in its job of surviving and reproducing, just as changes accidentally introduced into any artificial mechanism are predominantly harmful to its useful operations . . . good ones are so rare that we can consider them all bad.[45]

J.J. Fried wrote in *The Mystery of Heredity*:

> We have to face one particular fact, one so peculiar that in the opinion of some people it makes nonsense of the whole theory of evolution: Although the biological theory calls for incorporation of beneficial variants in the living populations, a vast majority of the mutants observed in any organism are detrimental to welfare. Some are lethal, causing incurable diseases or fatal deaths; others are sub-lethal killing off or incapacitating most of the carriers but allowing some to escape; still others are sub-vital, damaging health, resistance or vigor in a variety of ways.[46]

To mutate from a lower form of life to a higher form of life would require an exponentially large number of positive mutations. Not only is there not enough time in the proposed 3.5 billion year life of evolutionary activity on earth, Dr. Pierre-Paul Grassé of the University of Paris and past-president of the French Academy of Science states:

> The mass evidence shows that all, or almost all, known mutations are unmistakably pathological and the few remaining ones are highly suspect.[47]

Mutations do not produce new information or superior creatures. No scientific evidence exists to the contrary. A more nagging problem to the Darwin theory is the further realization that most mutant genes produce sterile offspring, incapable of passing on their "new" genetic information to others.

What Good Is Half a Wing?

An additional challenge: For natural selection to work, the new feature must be superior to the former one. But mutation-induced changes occur only incrementally. If the new feature is incomplete and functionless,

Can this bird fly?

the creature will be less likely to survive. Hence, no natural selection takes place. Dr. Colin Patterson, chief paleontologist at the British Museum of Natural History, points out this large obstacle to the concept of natural selection:

> The adaptive value of the perfected structure is easily seen, but intermediate steps seem to be useless, or even harmful. For example, what use is a lens in the eye unless it works? A distorting lens might be worse than no lens at all. . . . How can the segments of an animal like the earthworm or centipede arise bit-by-bit? An animal is either segmented or it is not. The usual answer to such a question is that they are due only to the failure of the imagination.[48]

Dr. Stephen J. Gould, evolutionary paleontologist, agrees:

> But how do you get from nothing such an elaborate something if evolution must proceed through a long sequence of intermediate stages, each favored by natural selection? You can't fly with 2% of a wing or gain much protection from an iota's similarity with a potentially concealing piece of vegetation. How, in other words, can natural selection explain these incipient stages of structures that can only be used (as we now observe them) in much elaborated forms? . . . One point stands high above the rest: the dilemma of incipient stages. Mivart identified this problem as primary and it remains so today.[49]

Gould further explains this convincing argument against gradual change:

> Even though we have no direct evidence for smooth transitions, can we invent a reasonable sequence of intermediate forms, that is, viable, functioning organisms, between ancestors and descendants? Of what possible use are the imperfect incipient stages of useful structures? What good is half a jaw or half a wing?[50]

His logical argument is that slow, evolutionary changes from one form into another is not possible, for one thing, because the transitional forms, being incomplete, would not be useful to the creature. What function could be served by only half an eye or half a leg? Such a creature would be clearly at a disadvantage, and would be unlikely to survive.

Transition forms are nonfunctional, or poorly functional, at best. Therefore, natural selection would not have favored their survival.

Darwin and his modern adherents teach that countless trillions of good mutations (accidental alterations of an organism's genetic code) would eventually produce complex species more fit for survival in a given environment. Aided by 160 years of extensive study since Darwin described his formula, science has proved the exact opposite to be true. The number of respected scientists to publicly question Darwin's theory is growing:

Dr. I. L. Cohen states:

> To propose and argue that mutations even tandem with "natural selection" are the root causes for 6,000,000 viable, enormously complex species is to mock logic, deny the weight of evidence, and reflect the fundamentals of mathematical probability.[51]

Natural selection does at times take place, but only on a very limited scale. Many species, dinosaurs for example, have become extinct over the years — a feature of natural selection. It is understandable that the fastest, most agile, and strongest creatures will survive longer than the sick, the weak, and the crippled. But while natural selection may explain the survival of the fittest within a particular group of plants or animals, it does not explain transformation from one species into another. Dr. Cohen explains:

> No one has ever produced a species by mechanisms of natural selection. No one has ever gotten near it.[52]

Dr. Pierre-Paul Grassé, the scientist who held the Chair of Evolution at the Sorbonne in Paris for 20 years, adamantly affirms that:

> No matter how numerous they may be, mutations do not produce any kind of evolution. The opportune appearance of mutations permitting animals and plants to meet their needs seems hard to believe. Yet the Darwinian theory is even more demanding. A single plant or a single animal would require thousands and thousands of lucky, appropriate events. Thus, miracles would become the rule: events with infinitesimal probability could no longer fail to occur. . . . There is no law against day dreaming, but science must not indulge in it.[53]

Dr. George G. Simpson, an American champion of evolutionary dogma, admitted that if there was an effective breeding population of say, 100 million individuals, and they could produce a new generation every single day, the likelihood of obtaining good evolutionary results from mutations could be expected only about once in 274 billion years. This, needless to say, is beyond the evolutionists' currently estimated 4.5 billion-year-old earth![54]

EYEING THE MATTER

Darwin himself further described the unlikelihood of mutation and natural selection producing new organ systems and new species. His self-doubt showed its face vividly when he furiously questioned his own theory with statements like this in his *The Origin of Species*:

> To suppose that the eye with all its inimitable contrivances for adjusting the focus to different distances, for admitting different amounts of light, and for the correction of spherical and chromatic aberration, could have been formed by natural selection, seems, I freely confess, absurd in the highest sense.[55]

> Darwin must have begun to realize the impossibility of his own theory. The eye, he initially proposed, evolved from a hole in the head all the way to an organ far more sophisticated than the most modern camera! The human eye has automatic aiming mechanism, automatic focusing, and automatic aperture adjustment. It can function in almost total darkness one moment, and in bright sunlight the next. And while we sleep, our eyes perform their own maintenance work! And this all happened by chance? Not![56]

Natural selection demands that a slight mutation make the creature more likely to survive. But the eye would have been useless without its complete system. Vision requires everything to be functioning, including the lens, retinal cells, optic nerves, and brain vision centers. Every component is essential. If any is lacking, vision (accompanied by increased survival) is impossible. Therefore, the eye could not possibly have evolved through natural selection.

G. Hardin expressed the logic in this reasoning when he wrote:

> How then are we to account for the evolution of such a complicated organ as the eye? . . . If even the slightest thing is wrong

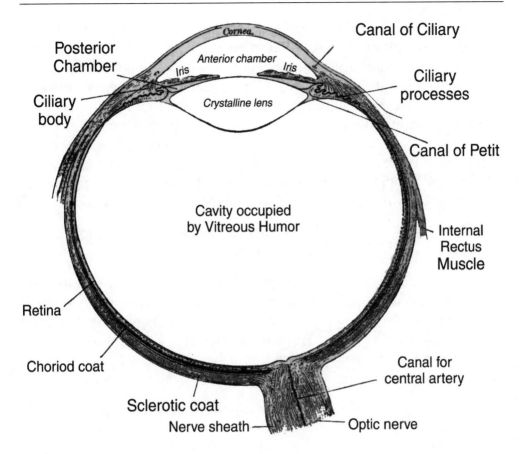

A horizontal section of the eyeball, an extremely complex structure.

— if the retina is missing, or the lens opaque, or the dimensions in error — the eye fails to form a recognizable image and is consequently useless. Since it must be either perfect, or perfectly useless, how could it have evolved by small, successive, Darwinian steps?[57]

AGAINST ALL ODDS

Evolution via random mutations from one species to another is scientifically impossible. Yet our biology classes and textbooks still teach, for example, that the modern bird evolved gradually from a lizard or members of the reptile family. Scientific reason categorically disagrees.

Random mutation and natural selection, among other things, would take immeasurable quantities of time. One proposal to get around this fact would be for creatures to suddenly make leaps in development. Harvard's revered evolutionist Dr. Stephen J. Gould entertained the possibility that one time a lizard egg hatched and out popped the first bird — so called "punctuated equilibrium." Dr. Gould proposed that all the mutations simply occurred in one creature at the same time, and at birth it became a new species. Sound like a reasonable possibility? What about the fact that a second bird of the opposite sex also must have hatched in the next nest in order for the new species to reproduce itself? Nevertheless, Gould insists:

> Major structural transitions can occur rapidly without a smooth series of intermediate stages.[58]

Punctuated equilibria, this new scenario for biological evolution, is sometimes called "hopeful monsters." However attractive the concept is for explaining the missing transition forms, the idea is nonsense. No speck of evidence has been found to support punctuated equilibria. Instead, those still holding to the theory of evolution concur with Dr. Robert Jastrow, NASA Science Director:

> It is the nature of biological evolution that it always proceeds slowly.[59]

EVIDENCE ON TRIAL

How do evolutionists deal with the evidence against their position? One option is to hide their inconsistencies. In his book *The Bone Peddlers*, William Fix opens the evolutionist's secret tomb:

> Scientists at the forefront of inquiry have put the knife to classical Darwinism. They have not gone public with this news, but have kept it in their technical papers and inner counsels.[60]

Or evolutionists sometimes laugh at the audacity of their own theory, as does Princeton professor of biology Dr. Edwin Conklin, in this commentary:

> The probability of life originating from accident is comparable to the probability of the unabridged dictionary resulting from an explosion in a printing shop.[61]

Another option is to simply decide to believe the unbelievable, as declared by Dr. George Wald, a professor emeritus of biology at Harvard and the Nobel Prize winner in biology in 1971:

> There are only two possible explanations as to how life arose: Spontaneous generation arising to evolution or a supernatural creative act of God. . . . There is no other possibility. Spontaneous generation was scientifically disproved 120 years ago by Louis Pasteur and others, but that just leaves us with only one other possibility . . . that life came as a supernatural act of creation by God, but I can't accept that philosophy because I do not want to believe in God. Therefore I choose to believe in that which I know is scientifically impossible, spontaneous generation leading to evolution.[62]

Scientists have attempted for years to engineer natural selection in the laboratory, under carefully controlled conditions. If successful at least under artificial circumstances, it might lend support to the idea of natural selection in nature. What have they found? Michael Pitman, former chemistry professor at Cambridge, confessed:

> Neither observation nor controlled experiment has shown natural selection manipulating mutations so as to produce a new gene, hormone, enzyme system or organ.[63]

What about employing simple honesty to deal with the facts of evolution? Stepping forward like the NBA All-Stars from the ranks of the world's most distinguished scientists are a growing number of outspoken evolutionists who accurately voice deep concerns over current evolutionary theory as presented as fact in modern textbooks.

Dr. Colin Patterson, senior paleontologist for the British Museum of Natural History, one of the world's leading evolutionists, and regarded as the world's foremost fossil scientist, takes such a stand:

> The explanation value of the evolutionary hypothesis of common origin is nil! Evolution not only conveys no knowledge, it seems to convey anti-knowledge. How could I work on evolution ten years and learn nothing from it? Most of you in this room will have to admit that in the last ten years we have seen the basis of evolution go from fact to faith! It does seem that the level of

knowledge about evolution is remarkably shallow. We know it ought not be taught in high school, and that's all we know about it.[64]

Dr. Wolfgang Smith, himself a physicist and mathematician, sees honesty beginning to prevail:

> A growing number of respectable scientists are defecting from the evolutionist camp . . . moreover, for the most part these "experts" have abandoned Darwinism, not on the basis of religious faith or biblical persuasions, but on strictly scientific grounds, and in some instances, regretfully.[65]

In spite of these doubts and defections, the public is still taught evolution as a fact of life. Arthur Koestler observes:

> In the meantime, the educated public continues to believe that Darwin has provided all the relevant answers by the magic formula of random mutations plus natural selection — quite unaware of the fact that random mutations turned out to be irrelevant and natural selection a tautology.[66]

Clearly, the public has been misled about the scientific support for evolution, including the components of random mutation and natural selection. Dr. I.L. Cohen calls it all a false theory:

> Micro mutations do occur, but the theory that these alone can account for evolutionary change is either falsified or else it is an unfalsifiable, hence metaphysical, theory. I suppose that nobody will deny that it is a great misfortune if an entire branch of science becomes addicted to a false theory. But this is what happened in biology: . . . I believe that one day the Darwinian myth will be ranked the greatest deceit in the history of science. When this happens, many people will pose the question: "How did this ever happen?"[67]

SUMMING UP

All living things are characterized by incredible specified complexity, meaning that their structures are so intricate that they could not possibly happen by chance. The genetic code of our DNA, for example, is elaborate beyond description. What's more, there are no "simple" cells. Even the most tiny one-celled creature is vastly complex and requires extremely elaborate DNA coding to be able to function and reproduce. Far greater still are the intricacies of human genetics and cellular functions.

Evolution first requires an intact, living, self-reproducing creature. And this requires spontaneous generation — life arising from dead material. However, research shows that the odds are virtually zero that all the necessary structures and chemicals randomly came together at the same instant, that the simplest cell could have formed by chance. What Louis Pasteur proved over a century ago is still true: non-life cannot produce life.

Given that the first living cell had spontaneously started, evolution says that it became more varied with each reproduction due to random genetic mutations. Some of these mutations made the creature stronger and better able to survive. These creatures, over time, varied so much that they became entirely new species.

However, progress from simple creatures to complex ones via random mutations and natural selection is scientifically impossible. Today we know that random mutations are actually rare events. They almost always kill the creature, or at least make it incapable of reproducing.

Furthermore, slight improvement wouldn't make a creature more likely to survive. For a creature to get any benefit from a new wing, for example, requires the new structure to be fully functioning. Natural selection does not favor a creature with a useless, underdeveloped wing. It is not likely to survive, putting an end to any hope of evolutionary development. A growing number of scientists are going public with these truths about the theory of evolution.

ENDNOTES

1 Leslie Orgel, *The Origins of Life* (New York, NY: John Wiley, 1973), p. 189.

2 Richard Dawkins, *The Blind Watchmaker* (New York, NY: W.W. Norton, 1986), p. 115.

3 Werner Gitt, "Dazzling Design in Miniature," *Creation Ex Nihilo*, 20(1):6 (December 1997–February 1998).

4 Henry Morris and Gary Parker, *What is Creation Science?* (Master Books: Green Forest, AR, 1987), p. 52–61.

5 *New Scientist*, 160(2154):23, (October 3, 1998), citing *Proceedings of the National Academy of Sciences*, 95:11, 804.

6 Michael Behe, *Darwin's Black Box: The Biochemical Challenge to Evolution* (New York, NY: The Free Press, 1996).

7 C.M. Fraser et. al., "The Minimal Gene Complement of Mycoplasma Genitalium," *Science*, 270(5235):397–403 (October 20, 1995) and *Perspective by A. Goffeau*, "Life With 482 Genes," same issue, p. 445–446.

8 W. Wells, "Taking Life to Bits," *New Scientist*, 155(2095):30-33, (1997).

9 Michael Denton, *Evolution: A Theory in Crisis* (Chevy Chase, MD: Adler and Adler Publishers, Inc., 1986).

10 William Beck, *Human Design* (New York, NY: Harcourt, Brace, Jovanovich, 1971).

11 Bert Thompson, *Creation Compromises* (Montgomery, AL: Apologetics Press, Inc. 1995).

12 Carl Sagan, Encyclopedia Britannica, 10:894, (1974).

13 Thompson, *Creation Compromises*.

14 Alma E. Guinness, *ABC's of the Human Body* (Pleasantville, NY: Reader's Digest Association, 1987).

15 Ibid.

16 Ibid.

17 Regina Avraham, *The Circulatory System* (New York, NY: Chelsea House, 1989).

18 Carl Sagan, *Broca's Brain* (New York, NY: Random House, 1979).

19 Robert Jastrow, *The Enchanted Loom: Mind in the Universe* (New York, NY: Simon and Schuster 1981).

20 George F. Cahill, *Science Digest*, 89[3]:105, (1981).

21 Duane Gish, *Evolution: the Fossils Say No* (El Cajon, CA: Institute for Creation Research, 1995).

22 *Encyclopedia Britannica*, "Evolution" (1977).

23 S.E. Aw, "The Origin of Life: A Critique of Current Scientific Models," *Creation Ex Nihilo Technical Journal*, 10(3):300–314 (1996).

Jonathan D. Sarfati, "Self Replicating Enzymes?" *Creation Ex Nihilo Technical Journal*, 11(1):4–6 (1997).

W. R. Bird, *The Origin of Species: Revisited* (Nashville, TN: Thomas Nelson, Inc., 1991), Vol. 1, Part 3.

24 "Hoyle on Evolution", *Nature*, vol. 294 (November 12, 1981): p. 148.

25 Ibid., p. 527.

26 Paul S. Taylor, *Origins Answer Book* (Mesa, AZ: Eden Productions, 1990).

27 Harold Morowitz, *Energy Flow In Biology* (New York, NY: Academic Press, 1968).

28 John Billingham and Rudolf Pe, editors, *Communications With Extra-Terrestrial Intelligence* (New York, NY: Pergamon Press, 1973).

29 Emile Borel, *Probabilities and Life* (New York, NY: Dover Publications, 1962).

30 Taylor, *Origins Answer Book*.

31 Pierre-Paul Grassé (University of Paris and past president, French Acadamie des Sciences), *Evolution of Living Organisms* (New York, NY: Academic Press, 1977).

32 Taylor, *Origins Answer Book*.

33 Ibid.

34 Denton, *Evolution: A Theory in Crisis*.

35 Taylor, *Origins Answer Book*.

36 Ilya Prigogine et. al., "Thermodynamics of Evolution," *Physics Today*, p. 23 (Nov. 1972).

37 Jacques Monod, *Chance and Necessity* (New York, NY: Vintage Books, 1972).

38 Edward P. Tryon (professor of physics, City University of New York, USA), "What Made the World?" *New Scientist* (March 8, 1984): p. 14.

39 C.P. Martin, *American Scientist*, 41:100 (1953).

40 E. Mary, *Mathematical Challenges to the Neo-Darwinian Interpretation of Evolution*, edited by P.S. Moorhead and M.M. Kaplan (Philadelphia, PA: Wistar Institute Press, 1967), p. 50.

41 J.D. Sarfati, "Decoding and Editing Design: Double Sieve Enzymes," *Creation Ex Nihilo Technical Journal*, 13(1):5-7 (1999).

42 J. Knight, "Top Translator," *New Scientist*, 158(2130):15 (April 18, 1998).

43 L. Spetner, *Not by Chance* (Brooklyn, NY: The Judaica Press, Inc.), p. 131–132, 138, 143. See review in *Creation Ex Nihilo*, 20(l):50-51 (December 1997/February 1998).

44 W.J. ReMine, *The Biotic Message* (St. Paul, MN: St. Paul Science, 1993), chapter 8.

45 "How Radiation Changes the Genetic Constitution," *Bulletin of the Atomic Scientists*, vol. 11, no. 9 (November 1955), p. 331.

46 John J. Fried, *The Mystery of Heredity* (New York, NY: J. Day Co., 1971), p. 135–136.

47 Grassé, *Evolution of Living Organisms*, p. 170.

48 Colin Patterson, *Evolution* (London: British Museum of Natural History, 1978), p. 142.

49 "Not Necessarily a Wing," *Natural History*, vol. 94, no. 10 (October 1985): p. 12–13.

50 S.J. Gould, *Natural History*, 86(6): 22-30 (1977).

51 I.L. Cohen, *Darwin Was Wrong: A Study in Probabilities* (Greenvale, NY: New Research Publications, Inc., 1984), p. 81.

52 Wayne Jackson, *The Evolution Revolution* (Montgomery, AL: Apologetics Press, Inc. 1994), quoting Dr. Colin Patterson, in a radio interview with the Britsh Broadcasting Corporation on March 4, 1982.

53 Grassé, *Evolution of Living Organisms*, p. 88–103.

54 Wayne Jackson, *Creation, Evolution, and the Age of the Earth* (Stockton, CA: Courier Publications, 1989), p. 2., quoting George G. Simpson *The Major Features of Evolution* (New York, NY: Columbia University Press, 1953), p.96.

55 Charles Darwin, *The Origin of Species* (London: A.L. Burt, 1859), p. 170.

56 Scott Huse, *The Collapse of Evolution* (Grand Rapids, MI: Baker Book House, 1988), p. 71.

57 Garrett J. Hardin, *Nature and Man's Fate* (New York, NY: Rinehart, 1961), p. 72.

58 Jackson, *The Evolution Revolution*, quoting Stephen J. Gould, "The Return of Hopeful Monsters," *Natural History* (June/July 1977), p. 24.

59 Jackson, *The Evolution Revolution*, quoting Robert Jastrow, "Evolution: Selection for Perfection," *Science Digest*, 89 (11):86.

60 Jackson, *The Evolution Revolution*, quoting William Fix, *The Bone Peddlers* (New York, NY: MacMillan, 1984), p. 179–180.

61 Jackson, *The Evolution Revolution*, quoting Edwin Conklin, *Reader's Digest* (January 1963): p. 92.

62 George Wald, "Origin, Life and Evolution," *Scientific American* (1978).

63 Michael Pitman, *Adam and Evolution* (London: Rider, 1984), p. 67–68.

64 Address given at the American Museum of Natural History, November 5, 1981.

65 Taylor, *Origins Answer Book*, p. 107.

66 Arthur Koestelr, *Janus: A Summing Up* (New York, NY: Vintage Books, 1978), p. 185.

67 I.L. Cohen, *Darwinism: The Refutation of a Myth* (London: Croom Helmm, 1987), p. 422.

CHAPTER 3

NOT AS OLD AS YOU'VE BEEN TOLD

THE TALK IN THE ROCK

The true age of the earth is essential information. For evolution — from primitive one-celled creatures to modern humans — to have occurred would require (among many other things) an inhabitable earth that is trillions of years old. What evidence exists to support the true age of the earth? We'll consider several measuring techniques.

Examining sedimentary rock is helpful. Such rock is made by water depositing layers of solid material on the earth's surface as heavier elements drop to the bottom, and lighter ones remain at the top. The layer is cemented together by pressure from overlying earth and minerals dissolved within the water. While driving cars, we sometimes see the layers of sedimentary rock that were cut to make highways. They look like layers of blankets laid out on top of one another.

There are two ways such rock could be formed. The first is by a small amount of water depositing layers of dirt and sand over a long period of time. The second is by a vast amount of water making such deposits over a short period of time.

Sedimentation today usually occurs slowly, as small amounts of water deposit layers of dirt and sand in tiny quantities. This observation leads some scientists to presume that it has always been this way. The general theory that assumes sedimentation occurs as a constant rate is called uniformitarianism. If this constant rate has always been the case, then the layers of rock would

Sedimentary rock

indeed have taken enormous time to form. The great thickness of the sedimentary rocks under us is often used as evidence for a very old earth.

Experiments and observations also tell us that sedimentation and sedimentary rock can form very rapidly. Take the Mount St. Helens eruption as an example. Located in Washington state, this volcano deposited 25 feet of finely layered sediment around its base in just six hours.[1]

Furthermore, experiments by several different scientists show that differently sized particles within sediment can quickly sort themselves into layers like those found in sedimentary rock today.[2]

To these layers, add time and pressure from the earth above and the result is sedimentary rock.

Therefore another possible explanation for thick sedimentary rock is a catastrophic event — such as the huge, globe-covering flood described in Genesis. Such a flood could well have picked up huge quantities of sediment, deposited them, and led to the formation of today's sedimentary rock. In the process, many living things would have been quickly buried and become fossilized.

The argument that sedimentary rock alone proves an ancient earth is not reliable. It could just as easily have been formed very quickly by a great flood. More about this later.

To Become a Fossil, Speed Must Be Colossal!

Much sedimentary rock is filled with fossils. This gives us clues about how the rock was actually formed. When a plant or animal dies and lies on the ground, it quickly rots and decays. After a few weeks, often little remains of the creature. Within a few months, even the bones of a larger animal disintegrate.

For a fossil to form, the plant or animal must be buried very quickly by mud, volcanic dust, or another protecting substance. Otherwise, the creature would decompose or be eaten by worms or predators. Next, the minerals in the water, rock, and soil are absorbed by the buried body. Over time, the body becomes hard because it has been saturated with the minerals.

If sedimentary rock was formed by laying down dirt and sand over millions of years, then the remains of the living things would easily have rotted long before they were covered and fossilized. The only way to explain the presence of fossils within rock is for these plants and animals to have been buried very quickly. A slow dying-off period scenario is not possible.

All this suggests that sedimentary rock containing fossils must have been formed rapidly; and this means days or weeks, not millions of years. We have reliable evidence showing actual plants and animals which were buried quickly and became fossilized. The booklet *Stones and Bones*, for example, illustrates a seven-foot-long ichthyosaur (a fish-shaped marine reptile, now extinct) that became fossilized while giving birth. We've also found fossils of fish in the act of swallowing other fish.

Most striking is a fossilized tree trunk oriented vertically. It extends through several layers of sedimentary rock. Indeed, these layers must have all been laid down at the same time. Otherwise, if the upper layers had taken millions of years (or even more than one year) to form, the top of the tree would have decomposed long before it was encased in rock.[3]

The fact that we have so many fossils is in itself evidence for an event that rapidly buried them, such as a worldwide flood. Certainly enough water exists to produce a flood of such proportions. Recent calculations on the quality of water on earth show that if the surface of the planet were smooth, the earth would be entirely covered with water to a depth of 1.7 miles (2.7 km).[4]

In summary, the presence of fossils in sedimentary rock indicates that the rock was formed quickly. Rather than supporting an old earth, this finding suggests the planet is far younger than usually thought.

WHICH CAME FIRST?

Determining the true age of rocks and fossils is inexact at best. Many errors are due to a problem with circular reasoning, where one "fact" is based upon another, but neither fact is certain.

For example, when determining the age of certain rocks, geologists sometimes look for clues in the fossils contained in those rocks. If the paleontologists say that a creature lived a certain number of years ago, the geologists often give the rock that particular age.

And, when paleontologists are determining the age of certain fossils, they sometimes look at the strata of the rock where the fossils were found. If the geologists say that the rock is a certain age, the paleontologists give the fossil that particular age. There's a problem with this approach: Neither the age of the fossil, nor the age of the rock is certain. This issue is highlighted by several prominent scientists:

R.H. Rastall, lecturer in economic geology at Cambridge University, notes:

> It cannot be denied that from a strictly philosophical standpoint geologists are here arguing in a circle. The succession of organisms has been determined by a study of their remains embedded in the rocks, and the relative ages of the rocks are determined by the remains of organisms that they contain.[5]

J.E. O'Rourke, writing in the *American Journal of Science*, agrees with this analysis:

> The rocks do date the fossils, but the fossils date the rocks more accurately. Stratigraphy cannot avoid this kind of reasoning, if it insists on using only temporal concepts, because circularity is inherent in the derivation of time scales.[6]

Niles Eldredge, of the American Museum of Natural History in New York, sums up the issue:

> And this poses something of a problem: If we date the rocks by their fossils, how can we then turn around and talk about patterns of evolutionary change through time in the fossil record.[7]

This circular reasoning can be further illustrated like this: Many rocks are said to be millions of years old simply because they contain fossils of extinct creatures. Radiometric dating helps assign an age to the particular fossils. But as we'll see below, radiometric methods are highly unreliable. We simply can't prove the age of a rock by the fossils it contains.

And, many fossils are said to be millions of years old simply because they were found in deeper layers of sedimentary rock. But this line of reasoning is upset when we realize that sedimentary rock can be formed quickly.

In reality, neither the fossils, nor the rock, nor the combination of the two tell us exactly how old they actually are.

The Flood and the Mud

A massive flood is the only reasonable explanation for finding the number and size of fossils we find today within sedimentary rock worldwide. Most of us have seen the effects of floods. They are not pretty, for the water not only rises, but also has currents that carry mud and debris everywhere. Eventually, the water recedes and the debris is found settled in dry layers.

Genesis chapters 6 through 9 gives an accurate account of God's decision to bring on a worldwide flood. He gave Noah instructions to build an ark according to specifications: 450' long, 80' wide, and 45' high, with 1.5 million cubic feet of storage area (about ten freight trains each pulling 52 boxcars) and deck equal to about 20 basketball courts. Two of every species of air-breathing animal in the world today could be housed adequately in half of that space.[8]

Noah and his sons (and perhaps hired men) built the ark in 120 years (Gen. 6:3). Meanwhile, God caused the animals to "come to Noah," likely using the same amazing instinct that causes birds and other animals to migrate thousands of miles to a specifically determined spot. Noah, his family, and two of every species of animal were enclosed within the ark.

Then came the flood, with rain and roaring underwater currents. It flooded for 40 days and "on that day all the springs of the great deep burst forth, and the floodgates of the heavens were opened" (Gen. 7:11). All the mountains of the world were covered for 150 days. Finally, the waters began to recede.

Noah's flood (approximately 3,000–3,500 B.C.) was a worldwide catastrophe, unparalleled in the earth's history. Instantly, trillions of tons of mud, all vegetation and all animal life were tumultuously overturned as the water channels from under the earth and the water canopy above the

Noah's ark

earth collided to cover the earth with water to the extent of covering the tallest mountains by 15 cubits (Gen. 7:11-20). One cubit is about 15 inches.

After six months of flooding and terrestrial cataclysm — according to Psalm 104:6–8 — the mountains were raised and the valleys lowered as the earth, oceans, mountains, canyons, plains, and prairies we know today were formed. The ark was opened, and the people and animals left in pairs to repopulate the earth.

The impact of the flood is well described by Texas A&M microbiologist Dr. Bert Thompson:

> Vast animal graveyards and fossiliferous rubble shifts have been found worldwide. Evidence of a great, sudden, and recent water cataclysm, followed by a deep freeze, across the entire great north, accompanied by titanic hydraulic forces and crustal upheavals, burying a host of mammoths, mastodons, elephants, and other great beasts in a region which is now almost totally devoid of vegetation has been documented.
>
> Vast numbers of fossil trees and plants, standing erect, ob-

lique, and even inverted while piercing through successive beds of water-laid stone have been discovered. There is abundant evidence of profuse vegetation and a temperate, even subtropical climate prevailing in Antarctica and the north polar regions at some time in the past.

Worldwide fossilization has occurred in vast quantities, including fossils in sedimentary strata, often at great depths and under great pressure. Vast and numerous rifts, fissures, and lava beds have been discovered, scarring the world ocean floor, all clearly recent and speak of some gigantic submarine upheaval of the earth's crust (as in breaking up of the "fountains of the deep"). Marine fossils have been found buried and exposed at almost every altitude. And on and on and on such evidences could be listed.[9]

Remnants of this worldwide flood can be found all over the earth. Marine crustaceans have been discovered on 12,000-foot high mountaintops. Hippopotamuses, living only in Africa, have been uncovered in England. Hundreds of dinosaurs have been found buried together with other creatures that did not share the same habitat. The Norfolk forest-beds in England contain fossils of northern cold-climate animals, tropical warm climate animals, and temperate zone plants all mixed together.

Search the earth and you will find the moose-deer (native of America) buried in Ireland; elephants (natives of Asia and Africa) buried in the midst of England; crocodiles (natives of the Nile) in the heart of Germany; shellfish (never known in the American seas) together with the entire skeletons of whales in the most inland regions of England.[10]

A whale's skeleton was even found on top of the Sanhorn Mountain , which is 3,000 feet high! Nothing could have conveyed the whale to that height except a great flood.[11]

Sea fossils are found on all the mountains of the world. Pillow lava is formed only under water. How did such diverse creatures get buried thousands of miles from their normal environments, at unexplainable elevation, except by a devastating universal flood? What's more, geologists have found a field of pillow lava as high as 15,000 feet on Mount Ararat.

The flood was so cataclysmic and so geologically impacting and climate-altering that it gives the best explanation in all of science for the tens of thousands of fossils buried instantly on all seven continents. It also helps explain coal formation, oil formation, canyon formation, and global climate changes (such as ancient warm humid marshes now being dug up from under deserts) now evident in various places from pole to pole.

The universal worldwide flood is not described in the Bible alone. Sir J. William Dawon, the famous Canadian geologist, writes:

> Further, we know that the deluge of Noah is not mere myth or fancy of primitive man or solely a doctrine of the Hebrew scriptures. The record of the catastrophe is preserved in some of the oldest historical documents of several distinct races of men, and is indirectly corroborated by the whole tenor of the early history of most of the civilized races.[12]

Dr. Bert Thompson also documents historical records of the flood:

> The account of the Genesis flood hardly stands alone. Researchers have described over 100 flood traditions from Europe, Asia, Australia, the East Indies, the Americas, East Africa, and many other places. Almost all accounts agree on these points:

> universal, worldwide flood
> all mankind perished
> an ark
> a seed of mankind survived to perpetuate the human race.[13]

The creation of fossilized creatures all over the world and the widespread rock layers are both explained by the violent and then slowly settling flood. Byron Nelson writes:

> A stream moving from side to side, or alternately fast and slow over one area for several hours or days would inevitably sort its material and deposit it in horizontal layers one above another, and we do not see what else could possibly do so.[14]

Noah's flood readily explains the finding of fossils in sedimentary rock, and also supports rapid formation of that rock. These both point to a young planet indeed.

WHAT HAPPENED TO THE DINOSAURS?

Evolutionists maintain that dinosaurs lived over 70 million years ago, and died out at least 60 million years before humans evolved. According to the Genesis account, however, humans and dinosaurs were created at the

same time, and therefore lived together. This is consistent with some little-publicized facts, such as:

- Discoveries have been made of cave-dwelling humans with drawings and carvings of dinosaurs on the walls of caves in Arizona's Hava Supai Canyon, and in 30 other places worldwide.
- Fossilized footprints of man and footprints of dinosaurs have been found in the same geological strata in New Mexico, Arizona, Mexico, Kentucky, Missouri, Russia, Illinois, Texas, and other locations![15]
- On March 16, 1982, in Glen Rose, Texas, Dr. Baugh, accompanied by other scientists, removed a layer of limestone 12 inches thick to reveal human and dinosaur prints within inches of each other! By the next day, they had uncovered four more human footprints and 23 more dinosaur prints all next to one another![16]

What's more, the Bible describes an eyewitness account of an ancient behemoth (dinosaur). The author of this book is believed to have lived about 3,500 years ago. Note the accurate description of the animal, with special attention to the description of the animal's tail. Although some skeptics have tried to classify this animal as a modern-day elephant or rhinoceros, the claim is preposterous, as no such animal has a tail that sways back and forth "like a cedar tree."

> Look at the behemoth, which I made along with you and which feeds on grass like an ox. What strength he has in his loins, what power in the muscles of his belly! His tail sways like a cedar; the sinews of his thighs are close-knit. His bones are tubes of bronze, his limbs like rods of iron (Job 40:15–18).

Many believe the "dragons" mentioned in the Bible (at least 25 times) were the dinosaurs of paleontology. This evidence indicates that dinosaurs, created at the same time as humans, lived together with them.

Then what happened to the dinosaurs? Many proposals have been put forward: epidemic disease, starvation, poison plants, even constipation. Another suggestion appeared in the January 6, 1982, issue of the *Minneapolis (Minnesota) Tribune*: "The extinction of the dinosaurs may have been caused by a giant asteroid that slammed into the earth 65 million years ago. The asteroid collision kicked up a huge cloud of dust containing iridium. The dust obscured the sun for three to six months, destroying the plants on which the dinosaurs fed."

Intriguing as they may sound, no substantial scientific evidence exists to support any of these proposals. Prior to the Flood, it's likely that the earth's worldwide climate was subtropical under the "water canopy" or dense clouds. Evidence suggests that after the Flood, most of the earth was significantly cooler than before. The dinosaurs on the ark (probably very young dinosaurs!) left to a completely new and milder climate. Unable to adjust to the temperature and changes in vegetation, many of their species died and became extinct.

A Radiometric Date May Make You Late

One of the best-known ways of assigning age to an object is through several techniques known jointly as radiometric dating. One method — radiocarbon dating — is especially designed to date fossils of living things.

Radiometric dating is based on the fact that some radioactive elements undergo decay to produce new elements. In the case of uranium-lead dating, uranium 238 (the "parent element") will eventually decompose to produce lead 206 (the "daughter element"). Scientists can measure the quantities of radioactive elements in rocks today, and estimate how long it's been since the rock cooled from its molten state. This gives an "age" for the rock.

Dr. Willard F. Libby invented the carbon 14 dating method, and developed it in the late 1940s and early 1950s. He won a Nobel Prize for chemistry. He said in his own book, however, that carbon 14 dating is only accurate to about 4,000 years. After that amount of time, the system becomes unreliable.[17]

In spite of its limitations, scientists have "sworn by" radiometric dating methods for the rocks that encase fossils and many other "ancient" objects. Are these dates truly reliable? Actually, radiometric dating is based on some fragile assumptions. If the assumptions are false, the dating procedure is worthless. For radiometric dating to be accurate several critical factors must be known or be true:

1. We must know the quantity of radioactive elements which were in the rock when it was first formed.
2. The rate of radioactive decay must be constant over time.
3. The rocks being measured must be insulated from outside factors.

These factors can be illustrated in the following way. Imagine yourself being a police investigator. You have discovered an abandoned car used in a robbery. To help identify the thief's hideout, you need to figure how far the car had been driven. First, you measure the amount of gasoline in the tank right now. But to answer the question, you must also consider three other factors, each corresponding to the radiometric facts above:

1. How much gasoline was in the tank when it left the hideout?
2. What is the car's fuel consumption rate in miles per gallon?
3. Does the tank have a fuel leak, or has any fuel been added since leaving the hideout?

As the police investigator, you will likely have a hard time pinning down the distance to the thief's hideout. Why? Because the information you need, especially questions 1) and 3), is likely impossible to know.

Similarly, the accuracy of radiometric dating is questionable in these same three critical factors:

1. We must know the quantity of radioactive elements that were in the rock when it was first formed.

BUT: It is impossible to know the quantity of radioactive elements in a rock when it was first formed, whether thousands, millions, or billions of years ago. We can only speculate. In most calculations, it is assumed that no daughter element was present when the rock formed, but there is no way to prove this. We also know from recently "created" rock from lava flow that this assumption is invalid. Sometimes the daughter element is already present.

2. The rate of radioactive decay must be constant over time.

BUT: Current evidence suggests that radioactive decay is indeed constant, and is not affected by heat or pressure. However, decay rates have been examined for only about 100 years. Nuclear physicist Dr. Russell Humphreys demonstrates research known as radiohalo analysis that suggests that decay rates used to be faster.

Dr. Kenneth L. Currie of the Canadian Geological Survey, notes that radioactive decay rates may not be constant:

> Natural processes in general do not act at fixed rates. The assumption that an average rate taken over a long period of time can be extrapolated is generally unsatisfactory.[18]

Frederic B. Jueneman stated in an article from the reputable journal *Industrial Research and Development*:

> There has been in recent years the horrible realization that radio decay rates are not as constant as previously thought, nor are they immune to environmental influences.[19]

We have no assurance what the radioactive decay rates were thousands, and certainly not billions, of years ago.

3. The rocks being measured must be insulated from outside factors.

BUT: Argon, one of the most measured radioactive elements, is a gas and can easily diffuse out of rock. Potassium and uranium (two other commonly measured elements) are easily dissolved in water. Water seeping among rock could easily dissolve away these elements, leading to inaccurate measurement. In reality, both parent and daughter elements migrate into the rocks from tectonic, metamorphic, and hydrologic forces. Geochronologists recognize this to be a serious and common problem to their dating method dogma.[20]

Though radiometric dating has been perfected for many years, the measurements are often very inaccurate. For example:

- Analysis of wood from Australia by the radiocarbon (14C) method revealed it to be 45,000 years old. But analysis by the potassium-argon method put the wood at about 45,000,000 million years old.[21]

- In another find, fossilized wood from Upper Permian rock layers was found to have radioactive carbon 14 present. The radiometric date assigned to these rock layers was 250,000,000. Yet other research reveals that all detectable carbon 14 should have disintegrated if the wood were older than 50,000 years.[22]

- A particular rock from Mount St. Helens volcano was obviously formed in 1986 when it cooled. But examination with the potassium-argon (K-Ar) radiometric method, determined it to be as 350,000 years old, give or take 50,000 years.[23]

- Newly formed rocks from the Mount Ngauruhoe volcano in New Zealand were also examined. The radiometric age of the rocks ranged between 270,000 and 3,500,000 years. However, these rocks were formed during eruptions between 1949 and 1975.[24]

Wakefield Dort Jr., of the department of geology at the University of Kansas, gives further examples:

> Radiocarbon analysis of specimens obtained from mummified seals in southern Victoria has yielded ages ranging from 615 to 4,600 years. A seal freshly killed at McMurdo had an apparent age of 1,300 years.[25]

Dr. Harold Slusher, an astrophysicist and geophysicist, adds:

> Studies on submarine basaltic rocks from Hawaii, known to have formed less than 200 years ago, when dated by the potassium-argon method, revealed "ages" from 160 million to almost 3 billion years.[26]

Dr. Alan C. Riggs, formerly of the U.S. Geological Survey and now on the staff of the University of Washington, Seattle, gives yet another example:

> By radiocarbon dating, living snails "died" 27,000 years ago![27]

So much for reliability! If radiometric dates are so unreliable for objects of known ages, then how can we trust the method for determining the age of unknown objects?

CALLING ON THE EXPERTS

Given these inaccuracies, it's no wonder that many scientists broadly question the usefulness of radiometric dating:

William D. Stansfield, Ph.D., instructor of biology at California Polytechnic State University, declares:

> It is obvious that radiometric techniques may not be the absolute dating methods that they are claimed to be. Age estimates on a given geological stratum by different radiometric methods are often quite different (sometimes by hundreds of millions of years). There is no absolutely reliable long-term radiological "clock." The uncertainties inherent in radiometric dating are disturbing to geologists and evolutionists.[28]

Richard L. Mauger, Ph.D., associate professor of geology at East Carolina University, admits with reference to radiometric dating:

> In general, dates in the "correct ball park" are assumed to be correct and are published, but those in disagreement with other data are seldom published nor are discrepancies fully explained.[29]

Robert E. Lee documents in "Radiocarbon: Ages in Error":

> The radiocarbon method is still not capable of yielding accurate and reliable results. There are gross discrepancies, the chronology is uneven and relative, and the accepted dates are actually selected dates. This whole blessed thing is nothing but 13th century alchemy, and it all depends upon which funny paper you read.[30]

T. Save-Soderbergh and I.U. Olsson, of the Institute of Egyptology and Institute of Physics (respectively) at the University of Uppsala, Sweden, make a confession of scientific bias:

> If a C-14 date supports our theories, we put it in the main text. If it does not entirely contradict them, we put it in a footnote. And if it is completely "out-of-date," we just drop it.[31]

Radiometric dating, long considered a secure means of determining age, must be viewed realistically. Its accuracy is highly unreliable. Yet this fact is seldom admitted. Current textbooks often present such views as proven facts. It is clearly time for parents to know the truth, for students to hear the truth, and for professors to teach the truth. Anything less is simply dishonesty.

NOT AS OLD AS YOU'VE BEEN TOLD

Numerous other methods have been used to determine the earth's true age. Taken as a whole, they give a more reliable indication. Consider some of them:

• Magnetic field intensity

The earth's magnetic field is rapidly decreasing in strength. Assessing the rate of decrease tells us about the planet's age. Dr. Thomas Barnes, one of the most respected magnetic field physicists in the world, explains:

> If we went back about ten thousand years, the earth's magnetic field would have been as strong as the field in a magnetic star. A magnetic star is like our sun; it has a nuclear power source. Surely our earth never had a nuclear source like the sun. Surely our earth never had a magnetic field stronger than that of a star. That would limit the age of the earth to ten thousand years.[32]

Calculations on the magnetic field by other investigators also reveal that it couldn't be more than about 10,000 years old.[33]

• Concentration of ocean salt

The concentration of salt in the oceans is steadily growing. Yet the oceans are not nearly salty enough to have existed for billions of years. Even with generous allowances, the salt concentration suggests they could be no more than 62 million years old at the most.[34]

• Preserved red blood cells

Preserved red blood cells and hemoglobin have been discovered in unfossilized dinosaur bones. Evolutionists dated the dinosaur as living 65 million years ago. However, research shows that such cells could not survive more than a few thousand years. The dinosaur must have lived recently.[35]

• Absent supernova

Supernova is the name given for the tremendous explosion of a star. It creates a brief light far brighter than any other object in a galaxy. Calculations show that the remains of supernovas continue shining for hundreds of thousands of years. Yet observations of our own Milky Way Galaxy do not show any old supernova. This fact suggests the galaxy has not existed long enough for these to have occurred.[36]

• Helium concentration

Helium concentration in our atmosphere is gradually increasing. Yet the current amount is only about 1/2000 of what we'd expect if the atmosphere were billions of years old. The helium concentration suggests a much younger atmosphere.[37]

• World Population Growth

World population growth is estimated by many population experts to be an average of about two percent per year. To be very conservative, if the population only increased one-half percent per year (allowing generously for plagues, wars, starvation, etc.), in one million years (the evolutionists general estimate of the age of man on planet Earth) there would have been 10^{2100} people somehow stacked on the earth. (That number of people would actually fill countless trillions of entire universes.) Even if an almost zero growth rate of population were assumed, in a million years the earth would have housed 3,000,000,000,000 people up until the present age. There is no cultural or fossil evidence for numbers anywhere near that level.

At the one-half percent growth rate, it would take about 4,000 years to produce today's population from a single couple. This is the approximate amount of time elapsed since the worldwide flood when only Noah's family was spared.

• Topsoil Depth

There is an average seven or eight inches of topsoil that sustains all of life on the earth, while the earth beneath the topsoil is as dead as rock. Scientists tell us that the combination of plants, bacterial decay and erosion will produce six inches of topsoil in 5,000 to 20,000 years. If the earth had been here for five billion years, we should have much more topsoil than the seven or eight inches; more on the order of 56 miles thick! It's a young world after all![38]

• Earth-moon distance

Measurements show that the moon is slowly withdrawing from the earth. Each year, the distance increases by about 1-1/2 inches, though the rate was likely greater in the past. Calculations show that even if the moon had been in contact with the earth, it would have taken only 1.37 billion years to reach its present distance. This gives a maximum possible age of the moon — not the actual age. This maximum age is still far too young for evolution to have had time to occur, and much younger than the radiometric "dates" assigned to moon rocks. Since the precise distance of the moon from the earth is critical for regulating ocean tides, the age must be a fraction of that amount of time.[39]

• Absent Meteorites

Where are the meteorites in the multi-billion-year-old geological column? While most meteors burn up before they reach the earth's surface, many (up to 60 tons each day) land on the earth. If the supposed geological layers were laid down over millions of years, where are the meteorites in the layers? No such meteors have been found in the geological layers.[40]

• "Short Period" Comets

Our solar system has an abundance of "short period" comets, that is, comets whose life span averages only 1,500 to 10,000 years. Yet if the universe is billions of years old, these comets would have disintegrated long ago. Evolutionists have had to scramble to try and explain their existence.[41]

• Our Shrinking, Self-Consuming Sun

It just makes sense to suspect that as the sun burns its fuel, the sun gets smaller. This can give us clues about its true age. Dr. John A. Eddy, an astrophysicist at the Harvard-Smithsonian High Altitude Observatory in Boulder, Colorado, observes:

> I suspect . . . that the sun is 4.5 billion years old. However, given some new and unexpected results to the contrary and some time for frantic adjustment, I suspect that we could live with Bishop Ussher's figure for the age of the earth and sun (approximately six thousand years). I don't think we have much in the way of observational evidence in astronomy to conflict with that.[45]

Dozens of independent studies from the Royal Greenwich Observatory and studies done independently at the U.S. Naval Observatory suggest that the sun's diameter is shrinking at the rate of six feet per hour. Dr. Eddy's studies suggest a solar diameter shrinkage of approximately ten miles per year.

The following scientists and scientific authors document studies that indicate the sun's shrinking rate:

D.W. Dunham	S. Sophia
A.D. Fiala	J. O'Keefe
J.R. Lesh	A.S. Endal
Andrew A. Snelling	Dudley J. Benton
Thomas G. Barnes	Paul D. Ackerman
Harold L. Armstrong	Paul M. Steidl
Ronald L. Gillilland	David D. Dunham
Hilton Hinderliter	John Eddy
G. Russell Akridge	

Dennis Petersen applies this information to its logical conclusion:

> If the sun existed only 100,000 years ago it would have been double its present diameter. And only twenty million years ago the surface of the sun would be touching the earth.[46]

How does one reconcile the earth being billions of years old, and yet the sun being in contact with the earth only 20 million years ago? What's more, over 99.8 percent of the earth's supposed multi-billion-year history, the earth would have been exponentially too hot to support any hope for life.[47]

AGE IS NO REQUIREMENT

Looking for other evidence of the earth's age? Petrified objects, the formation of coal, coral reefs, and the Grand Canyon are also said to prove a very old earth. But recent discoveries make these arguments more difficult to support. Instead, they all point toward the probability of a young planet:

• Petrifaction

The time necessary for wood and other objects to become petrified is said to be on the order of thousands of years. But consider the findings of H.G. Labudda of Kingaroy in southeast Queensland, Australia, who specializes in the collection of petrified objects. Among the articles of his collection is a perfectly petrified orange. Oranges were not raised in the area until 1868.[48]

The solar system

• Coal Formation

In many places are fossilized trees penetrating through several coal layers. This indicates that the surrounding coal was formed so quickly that termites did not have time to consume the wood! Rather than taking millions of years to form coal, E.S. Moore, a coal geologist, declares:

> From all available evidence it would appear that coal may form in a very short time, geologically speaking, if conditions are favorable.[49]

• Coral Formation

Coral is said to grow only slowly, and that reefs take millions of years to form. Yet underwater explorers recently found a five-foot diameter coral growth on the bow gun of a sunken ship. Coral can indeed grow much more rapidly than previously thought.[50]

• Canyon Formation

Some geologists have declared that, given its depth, the Grand Canyon and other geological strata must have taken more than one billion years to form. However, we know today that some comparatively small "natural disasters" can have the same affect much more quickly.

On March 19, 1982, Mount St. Helens' exploded with the force equaled by 20,000 Hiroshima-sized atom bombs. As an aftermath of the eruption, a 140-feet-deep canyon (the "Little Grand Canyon") was formed in just one day! At this rate, the Grand Canyon could have been formed in only 40 days!

Since the eruption, new rock layered strata (like walls of the Grand Canyon) have also continued to form at the rate of 100 feet per year (in one case 25 feet in one day).[51]

Furthermore, the walls of the Grand Canyon reach over 6,000 feet above sea level. The river that supposedly "carved" these walls "billions of years ago" enters the canyon at only 2,800 feet above sea level. Rivers don't flow uphill! To "carve" those walls, the river would have had to flow uphill over 3,200 feet vertically! Clearly, the river did not form the Grand Canyon!

Eastern Washington has its "channeled scablands" — 15,000 square miles of steep-walled canyons, gouged out of crystalline lava rock. Researchers initially assumed these canyons were the aftermath of a river eroding the earth over many millions of years. United States Geological Survey, however, published the fact that the scablands were actually formed from the "Great Spokane Flood" in just two days!

WAIT! THERE IS STILL MORE!

There exist many other dating methods we have yet to touch on. The following are examples from a list of 102 dating methods that further suggest a very young earth and young universe:

> Volcanic activity of Jupiter's moon, Io
> Saturn's unstable rings
> The solar dust ring discovery
> Basaltic lunar craters
> The mystery of Sirius B
> The field-galaxy mystery
> Radiohalos
> Polonium Halos
> Chorine leaching
> Chorine influx
> Dust speed

Galaxy mass
Galaxy spirals
Helium in zircons
Lead in zircons
Lead influx
Sediment accumulation
Sediment lithification
Sodium leaching
Sodium influx
Strata unconsolidation
Strontium formation
Strontium influx
Uranium influx[52]

Studying these subjects presents considerable challenges to the idea of a very old earth. It is likely impossible to prove the earth's age using any one scientific method. This is because it is not feasible to have all the information needed from events that happened long ago. What we must do in these situations, scientifically speaking, is to gather as much data as possible and draw the best conclusions we honestly can.

The greatest weight of scientific evidence points toward a young earth. Not one in the "billions of years old" range, but rather consistent with a "thousands of years old" planet.

BIG BANG?

When further pondering the age of our planet, it's often taught that the universe began as a "big bang." Consider this statement from a high school textbook:

A fireball exploded 15 to 20 billion years ago. Then matter and energy spread outward in all directions, cooling as it expanded. After about 500,000 years, hydrogen gas formed. The gas collected into clouds which formed galaxies during the next half billion years. Now all that remains are galaxies and radiation. Within the galaxies, stars form and die and new ones form. . . . Probably the most widely accepted theory for the origin of the solar system is the dust cloud theory. According to this idea, a dust cloud began to rotate. . . . When the mass had swept up most of the material in an eddy, a planet was formed.[53]

Some scientists hold that the universe began with an incredible explosion of a very dense (1025 g/cc) sub-atomic particle, sometimes called the "cosmic egg." That explosion somehow resulted in a very vast, ordered universe (with over 100 billion galaxies), solar system, life-supporting planet Earth, and advanced forms of human life. The big-bang theory says that all this order resulted from the random effects of an explosion!

This theory is, however, scientifically impossible and intuitively unbelievable. Observations and experiments show that explosions always produce disorder and chaos. Nowhere in the universe has a single explosion been historically observed that produced higher order and greater complexity. This fact is summed up in the second law of thermodynamics:

> Complex ordered arrangements and systems naturally become simpler and more disorderly (increased entropy or randomness) with time.

This law is universal. Ordered arrangements (such as our solar system) also require a high degree of energy to maintain them. Yet, the second law also states that usable energy in the universe is becoming less and less as arrangements become more and more random. In a sense, the universe is like the constant unwinding of a great clock.

A "big bang" type of explosion always, always, always destroys complexity and produces disorder. Rather than forming planets and star systems, matter should have continued expanding and dissipated completely, for in outer space there is nothing to stop a moving object. Yet the universe demonstrates incredible order and design. The big-bang theory simply defies the laws of science and logic, yet is still clung to in spite of the facts.

What are the odds that such an explosion could produce the highly organized structures we see in the universe? Carl Sagan (himself an evolutionist and astronomer) gives it the immense odds of 1 to $10^{2,000,000,000}$ — that is 1 to 10 followed by two billion zeroes. Absolutely impossible![54]

Other profound questions are also left unanswered. What was the origin of the "cosmic egg" itself? Where did this first dense particle come from? From where was the enormous energy supplied? The big-bang theory has no answer to these essential queries, as voiced by A. Krauskopf and A. Beiser:

> A number of scientists are unhappy with the big bang theory.
> . . . For one thing, it leaves unanswered the questions that always

arise when a precise date is given for the creation of the universe: Where did the matter come from in the first place?[55]

What about the question of star light? To the astrophysicist, the universe looks very old. Traveling at incredible speed (186,000 miles per second), light we see today from distant stars had to travel millions or billions of years to get here. But if the universe is only a few thousand years old, how would light have time to reach us?

This problem is actually answered rather easily when you consider the law of general relativity discovered by Albert Einstein. One element of this law says that time is affected by gravity. In places of high gravity, time slows down. But in places of little or no gravity, time speeds up significantly. A clock on earth (high gravity) ticks more slowly than a clock in outer space (no gravity).

Light traveling in outer space covers distance faster in one earth year compared to light traveling within earth's own gravity. And the time experienced by the light particles themselves actually slows to almost zero at the speed they travel. Calculations show that because of these effects, we can indeed see light today from stars billions of light-years away, even though the light left those stars only thousands of years ago.[56]

BIG BUST!

Many scientists do not find sufficient evidence to support the big-bang theory. They judge its logic absurd and probability impossible. Some scientists in certain biased textbooks must "agree" with the theory to support the philosophical bias of their publisher, but in reality the scientists couldn't be more diametrically opposed.

Lemonick and Nash quote some authorities' misgivings with the big bang theory:

> "If we really trust the data," exclaims Stanford astrophysicist Andrei Linde, "then we are in disaster, and we must do something absolutely crazy. But this hasn't stopped the theorists from doing crazy things anyway; they've proposed one mind-stretching idea after another to explain what's going on."[57]

Leslie, an author and scientist, agrees that the logic is missing, saying:

> It is hard to see how galaxies could have formed in a universe which is flying apart so fast.[58]

Sir Fred Hoyle, British astronomer, nails the coffin shut on the big-bang theory:

> An explosion merely throws matter apart, while the big bang has mysteriously produced the opposite effect, with matter clumping together in the form of galaxies.[59]

Sir Hoyle also adds:

> The notion that galaxies form, to be followed by an active astronomical history, is an illusion. Nothing forms; the thing (the big-bang theory) is dead as a doornail.[60]

Renowned cosmologist John Gribbin expresses the conclusion of many others:

> Many cosmologists now feel that the shortcomings of the standard (big-bang) theory outweigh its usefulness.[61]

Any unbiased individual can tell you that explosives always produce chaos — not systems of extremely well-ordered, well-designed complexities like galaxies and solar systems. This fact led British astronomer Paul Davies to write:

> The greatest puzzle is where all the order in the universe came from originally.[62]

Davies, in a *New Scientist* journal article, concurs:

Everywhere we look in the universe, from the far-flung galaxies to the deepest recesses of the atom, we encounter order.[63]

Einstein also agreed, suggesting that the "high degree of order" was somewhat of a "miracle."[64]

What, then, is the most reasonable explanation for the complex structures of our universe? The big-bang theory is a big bust. The only possible explanation is this: The universe must have been designed and created that way!

IT'S ABOUT TIME!

How old is planet Earth? The question is essential. For evolution to be true requires an inhabitable planet "billions of years old" (actually, countless trillions of years old!) to give enough time for life to emerge and develop. Any time less, and evolution is impossible to support.

Everett Koop, former U.S. Surgeon General, vividly describes the challenge:

> When I make an incision with my scalpel, I see organs of such intricacy that there simply hasn't been enough time for natural evolutionary processes to have developed them.[65]

A great temptation faced by evolutionists is to stretch logic to the near breaking point, to assign old ages to fossils and other artifacts, when the scientific evidence is contrary. It's a very hard fact to confess, but more and more evolutionists are admitting the truth about our young earth:

Dr. Stephen Moorebath of the University of Oxford, an evolutionist himself, writes:

> No terrestrial rocks closely approaching an age of 4.6 billion years have yet been discovered. The evidence for the age of the earth is circumstantial, being based upon . . . indirect reasoning.[66]

Dr. Harold Slusher, an astrophysicist and geophysicist, also agrees:

> There are a number of indicators that seem to indicate an age of no more than 10,000 years, at the very most, for the solar system and the earth.[67]

Summing Up

An ancient, inhabitable earth is an absolute requirement for evolution to have time to occur. We've been taught that sedimentary rock indicates an old planet. Today, however, we know that sedimentary rock can actually form very quickly. A great worldwide flood can certainly explain many features we find in geology.

Radiometric dating, long considered a gold standard, is actually a flawed and unreliable technique. For accuracy, it requires information about the ancient world that we have no way of knowing today. Many other methods of estimating the earth's age, from studying our magnetic fields to the thickness of dust on the moon, point toward a very young planet.

What's more, evidence for the big bang, another cornerstone of the ancient earth idea, is shaky and contradicts the laws of physics. The order displayed by the universe could not possibly result from a massive explosion.

Contrary to what is commonly taught, the earth is not four to five billion years old. Scientific evidence actually supports a planet on the order of only six to ten thousand years old, far too young for evolution to have any chance to occur.

ENDNOTES

1 R.E. Walsh, editor, *Proceedings of the First International Conference on Creationism,* "Mount St. Helens and Catastrophism," by Stephen Austin (Pittsburgh, PA: Creation Science Fellowship, 1986).

2 P. Julien, Y. Lan, and G. Berthault, "Experiments on Stratification of Heterogeneous Sand Mixtures," *Creation Ex Nihilo Technical Journal,* 8(1):3750 (1994).
    H.A. Makse, S. Havlin, P.R. King, H.E. Stanley, "Spontaneous Stratification in Granular Mixtures," *Nature,* 386(6623):379–382 (March 27, 1997).

3 Carl Wieland, *Stones and Bones* (Green Forest, AR: Master Books, Inc., 1994).

4 R.A. Kerr, "Pathfinder Tells a Geologic Tale with One Starring Role," *Science,* 279(5348):175 (January 9, 1998).

5 R.H. Rastall (lecturer in economic geology, Cambridge University), Encyclopedia Britannica (1956), Vol. 10, p. 168.

6 J.E. O'Rourke, *American Journal of Science,* vol. 276 (January 1976): p. 53.

7 Niles Eldredge (American Museum of Natural History, New York), *Time Frames: The Rethinking of Darwinian Evolution and the Theory of Punctuated Equilibria* (New York, NY: Simon and Schuster, 1985 and London: William Heinemann, Ltd, 1986), p. 52.

8 Bert Thompson, *The Global Flood of Noah* (Montgomery, AL: Apologetics Press, 1986), p. 34–35.

9 Ibid., p. 44–45.

10 Byron Nelson, *The Deluge Story in Stone* (Minneapolis, MN: Augsburg Publishing House, 1968), p. 66.

11 Ibid., p. 85.

12 J. William Dawon, *The Historical Deluge in Relation to Scientific Discovery,* p. 4ff.

13 Thompson, *The Global Flood of Noah,* p. 13–14.

14 Nelson, *The Deluge Story in Stone,* p. 40.

15 *Los Angeles Herald Examiner,* January 7, 1970.

16 Carl E. Baugh and Clifford A. Wilson, *Dinosaur* (Orange, CA: Promise Pub., 1991), p. 11-12.

17 Wayne Jackson, *Creation, Evolution, and the Age of the Earth* (Stockton, CA: Courier Publications, 1989), p.13.

18 Jackson, *Creation, Evolution, and the Age of the Earth,* p. 10, quoting Kenneth L. Currie, *Rock Strata and the Biblical Record,* edited by Paul Zimmerman (St. Louis, MO: Concordia, 1970), p.70.

19 Frederic B. Jueneman, "Secular Catastrophism," *Industrial Research and Development* (June 1982): p. 21.

20 Jackson, *Creation, Evolution, and the Age of the Earth,* p. 8–9.

21 A.A. Snelling, "Radiometric Dating in Conflict," *Creation,* 20(1):24-27 (December 1997–February 1998).

22 A.A. Snelling, "Stumping Old-Age Dogma," *Creation,* 20(4):48-50 (September/November 1998).

23 S.A. Austin, "Excess Argon within Mineral Concentrates from the New Dacite Lava Dome at Mount St. Helens Volcano," *Creation Ex Nihilo Technical Journal,* 10(3):335343 (1986).

24 E. Walsh, editor, *Proceedings of the Fourth International Conference on Creationism*, "The Cause of Anomalous Potassium-Argon 'Ages' for Recent Andesite Flows at Mt. Ngauruhoe, New Zealand, and the Implications for Potassium-Argon 'Dating,' " by A.A. Snelling (Pittsburgh, PA: Creation Science Fellowship, 1998), p. 503–525.

25 Wakefield Dort Jr., "Mummified Seals of Southern Victoria Land," *Antarctic Journal* (Washington), vol. 6 (September–October 1971), p. 211.

26 William J.J. Glashouwer and Paul S. Taylor, "The Earth, a Young Planet," a film produced by Eden Communications, Gilbert, AZ, 1983.

27 Dr. Alan C. Riggs, "Major Carbon-14 Deficiency in Modern Snail Shells from Southern Nevada Springs," *Science*, vol. 224 (April 6,1984): p. 58.

28 William D. Stansfield, *The Science of Evolution* (New York, NY: MacMillan, 1977), p. 82, 84.

29 Richard L. Mauger, "K-Ar Ages of Biotites from Tuffs in Eocene Rocks of the Green River, Washakie, and Uinta Basins, Utah, Wyoming, and Colorado," *Contributions to Geology*, University of Wyoming, vol. 15(1), (1977): p. 37

30 Robert E. Lee, "Radiocarbon: Ages in Error," *Anthropological Journal of Canada*, vol. 19(3), (1981): p. 9–29.

31 Ingred U. Olsson, editor, *Radiocarbon Variations and Absolute Chronology, Proceedings of the Twelfth Nobel Symposium,* "C-14 Dating and Egyptian Chronology," by T. Save-Soderbergh and I.U. Olsson (Stockholm: Almqvist & Wiksell and New York: John Wiley & Sons, Inc., 1970), p. 35.

32 William J.J. Glashouwer and Taylor, "The Earth, A Young Planet?" quoting Thomas Barnes.

33 R.E. Walsh, editor, *Proceedings of the First International Conference on Creationism,* "Reversals of the Earth's Magnetic Field During the Genesis Flood," by D.R. Humphreys (Pittsburgh, PA: Creation Science Fellowship, 1986), Vol. 2, p. 113–126.

    J. D. Sarfati, "The Earth's Magnetic Field: Evidence That the Earth Is Young," *Creation*, 20(2):15-19 (March–May 1998).

34 R.E. Walsh, editor, *Proceedings of the Second International Conference on Creationism,* "The Sea's Missing Salt: A Dilemma for Evolutionists," by S.A. Austin and D.R. Humphreys (Pittsburgh, PA: The Fellowship, 1990), Vol. 2, p. 17–33.

    J.D. Sarfati, "Salty Seas: Evidence for a Young Earth," *Creation*, 21(l):16-17 (December 1998–February 1999).

35 C. Wieland, "Sensational Dinosaur Blood Report!" *Creation*, 19(4):42-43 (September–November 1997.)

    M. Schweitzer and T. Staedter, "The Real Jurassic Park," *Earth* (June 1997): p. 55–57.

36 R.E. Walsh, editor, *Proceedings of the Third International Conference on Creationism,* "Distribution of Supernova Remnants in the Galaxy," by K. Davies (Pittsburgh, PA: The Fellowship 1994), p. 175–184.

    J.D. Sarfati, "Exploding Stars Point to a Young Universe," *Creation*, 19(3):46-49 (June–August 1998.)

37 L. Vardiman, *The Age of the Earth's Atmosphere: A Study of the Helium Flux through the Atmosphere* (El Cajon, CA: Institute for Creation Research, 1990).

    J.D. Sarfati, "Blowing Old-Earth Belief Away: Helium Gives Evidence That the Earth Is Young," *Creation*, 20(3):19-2 1 (June–August 1998).

38 Edward Blick, *Correlation of the Bible and Science* (Oklahoma City, OK: Hearthstone Publishing, 1994), p. 28.

39 Don DeYoung, *Creation Ex Nihilo*, 14(4)43 (September–November 1992).

40 W.H. Twenhofel, *Principles of Sedimentation* (New York, NY: McGraw-Hill, 1950), second edition, p. 144.

    Walter T. Brown Jr., *In The Beginning* (Phoenix, AZ: Center for Scientific Creation, 1989), p. 53.

41 John Maddox, "Halley's Comet Is Quite Young," *Nature*, vol. 339 (May 11, 1989).

42 Paul D. Ackerman, *It's A Young World After All* (Grand Rapids, MI: Baker Book House, 1986), p. 22.

43 Raymond Arthur Lyttleton, *The Modern Universe* (London: Hodder and Stoughton, 1956), p. 72.

44 Isaac Asimov, "14 Million Tons of Dust Per Year," *Science Digest* (Jan. 1959): p. 36.

45 R.G. Kazmann, "It's About Time: 4.5 Billion Years" (report on symposium at Louisiana State University), *Geotimes*, vol. 23 (September 1978): p. 18, quoting John Eddy.

46 Dennis R. Petersen, *Unlocking the Mysteries of Creation* (El Dorado, CA: Creation Resource Foundation), p. 43.

47 Paul S. Taylor, *Origins Answer Book* (Mesa, AZ: Eden Productions, 1990), p. 68–69.

48 *Science* (August 16, 1963).

49 Glashouwer and Taylor, "The Earth, A Young Planet?" quoting Thomas Barnes.

50 Taylor, *Origins Answer Book*, p. 68–69.

51 Kazmann, "It's About Time: 4.5 Billion Years," p. 18, quoting John Eddy.

52 Taylor, *Origins Answer Book*, p. 69.
    Ackerman, *It's a Young World After All*.

53 Margaret Bishop, *Focus on Earth Science*, teacher's edition (Columbia, OH: Merrill, 1981), p. 470.

54 John Billingham and Rudolf Pe, editors, *Communications With Extra-Terrestrial Intelligence* (New York, NY: Pergamon Press, 1973).

55 Konrad B. Krauskopf and Arthur Beiser, *The Physical Universe* (New York, NY: McGraw-Hill, 1973), third edition, p. 645.

56 D. Russell Humphreys, *Starlight and Time* (Green Forest, AR: Master Books, 1994).

57 Michael D. Lemonick and J. Madeleine Nash, "Unraveling Universe," *Time* (March 6, 1995): p. 78.

58 N. Rescher, editor, *Scientific Explanation and Understanding*, "Cosmology, Probability, and the Need to Explain Life," by Leslie (Lanham, MD: University Press of America, 1983), p. 54.

59 Sir Fred Hoyle, *The Intelligent Universe* (New York, NY: Holt, Rinehart & Winston, 1983), p. 185.

60 Bert Thompson, *Cosmic Evolution and the Origin of Life* (Montgomery, Al: Apologetics Press, Inc., 1989), p. 7.

61 Ibid., p. 5, quoting John Gribbin, "Cosmologists Move Beyond the Big Bang," *New Scientist*, vol. 110, p. 30.

62 P. Davies, "Universe in Reverse — Can Time Run Backwards?" *Second Look* (Sept. 1979): p. 27.

63 Davies, "Chance or Choice: Is the Universe an Accident?" *New Scientist*, vol. 80 (1978): p. 506.

64 Albert Einstein, *Letters à Maurice Solovine* (Paris: Gauthier-Villars, 1956), p. 115.

65 Taylor, *Origins Answer Book*, p. 18–20.

66 Jackson, *Creation, Evolution, and the Age of the Earth*, p. 5, quoting Stephen Moorebath, *Scientific American* (March 1977): p. 92.

67 Glashouwer and Taylor, "The Earth, a Young Planet?" quoting Harold S. Slusher.

CHAPTER FOUR

THE REAL HARD ROCK

Fossils — The Real "Hard Rock"

Over the years, the earth's crust has stored up many fossils (remnants of living creatures whose bodies were encased and preserved). Conventional wisdom says that the "fossil record" occurred through the gradual laying down of fossils of one generation on top of those of the older generation. Therefore, when scientists dig downward they'd expect that the first fossils are the "newest." Those fossils farthest from the surface would likely be the oldest.

This record of layers and layers of fossils through both earth and time is known as the geologic column. Knowing at what depth a fossil is found (especially compared to other fossils around it) helps scientists to determine in what sequence creatures lived. Another key concept — uniformitarianism — says that the layers of earth and rock have been laid down at a uniform rate since time began.

Evolution proposes that living things very slowly transformed from one type into another. Therefore, we would expect to find fossils that show this transition, fossils of "intermediate" or "transitional" types of creatures. Sometimes these are referred to as "missing links."

For example, if reptiles transformed into birds over millions of years, we'd expect to find millions of fossils, say, of reptiles whose scales were becoming more feather-like, whose front legs were beginning to fan out like wings, and whose mouths were becoming pointed and beak-like.

Likewise, if apes very slowly transformed into humans, we'd expect to find millions of fossils of apes with progressively shorter arms, less body hair, smaller jaws, and larger heads.

SCIENTISTS AGREE: THE TALK IS IN THE ROCK

In analyzing evidence of evolution or creation we can utilize the fields of cosmology, physics, statistics, molecular biology, and genetics. Ultimately, however, what actually happened in the past can only be verified by examining the fossils. Numerous leading scientists agree.

Pierre Grassé, one of the most distinguished French zoologists, condemns the claim that fossils are not essential to support evolution:

> Naturalists must remember that the process of evolution is revealed only through fossil forms. A knowledge of paleontology is, therefore, a prerequisite; only paleontology can provide them with the evidence of evolution and reveal its course or mechanisms. Neither the examination of present beings, nor imagination, nor theories can serve as a substitute for paleontological documents. If they ignore them, biologists, the philosophers of nature, indulge in numerous commentaries and can only come up with hypotheses.[1]

Douglas Futuyma, in his book against evolution, also cuts to the core importance of checking out the fossils:

> Creation and evolution, between them, exhaust the possible explanations for the origin of living things. Organisms either appeared on the earth fully developed or they did not. If they did not, they must have developed from pre-existing species by some process of modification. If they did appear in a fully developed state, they must indeed have been created by some omnipotent intelligence.[2]

Evolutionists Glenister and Witzke agree with the fossil's vital importance:

> The fossil record affords an opportunity to choose between evolutionary and creationist models for the origin of the earth and its life forms.[3]

Short of studying the fossils, we are only left with speculation about what life was like in the distant past. If life arose from a lifeless world through an evolutionary process, if it became more complex and formed into millions of species, then the fossils actually found should illustrate this process.

But, if life came about because of special creation, the findings will be very different. Let's review what studying the fossils has revealed in some representative cases.

No Plants from Slime

What evidence has been found about the origin of flowering plants, also known as angiosperms? Darwin described their beginning as "an abominable mystery." From an evolutionary perspective, this mystery continues even today. Hughes describes several attempts to explain why evidence for their evolution cannot be found:

> The evolutionary origin of the now dominant land-plant group, the angiosperms, has puzzled scientists since the middle of the nineteenth century. . . . With few exceptions of detail, however, the failure to find a satisfactory explanation has persisted and many biologists have concluded that the problem is not capable of solution by fossil evidence.[4]

Fossils of flowering plants seem to have suddenly appeared in all their present-day variety. No trace has been found of more primitive plants developing into those more complex. When further considering the fossil evidence, Beck concludes:

> Indeed, the mystery of the origin and early evolution of the angiosperms is as pervasive and as fascinating today as it was when Darwin emphasized the problem in 1879. . . . We have no definitive answers, because we are forced to base our conclusions largely on circumstantial evidence, and they must usually, of necessity, be highly speculative and interpretative.[5]

By the word "speculative," Beck means that botanists may propose that one plant evolved from another, but that there is no evidence to prove this idea. Also challenged by the findings, Arnold describes the proof that he anticipated would be found in plant fossils:

It has long been hoped that extinct plants will ultimately reveal some of the stages through which existing groups have passed during the course of their development, but it must freely be admitted that this aspiration has been fulfilled to a very slight extent even though paleobotanical research has been in progress for more than one hundred years.[6]

Remarks of E.J.H. Comer of the Cambridge University School of Botany demonstrate fossil evidence for creation rather than evolution:

Much evidence can be adduced in favor of the theory of evolution from biology, biogeography, and paleontology, but I still think that to the unprejudiced, the fossil record of plants is in favor of special creation.[7]

The remarkable facts surrounding flowering plants are that they seem to have appeared suddenly, and in great variety. No traces of ancestors, intermediate forms, or missing links have been found among the fossils. To date, explaining their development in terms of evolution has been only a hypothesis. The proof has yet to be found.

No Bird from Lizard

Birds are animals well prepared for flight with unique features like feathers, hollow bones, and special lungs. Most evolutionists believe birds evolved from reptiles, maybe even a type of dinosaur. *Archaeopteryx* is thought by some to be an example of a transitional form: half-bird and half-reptile. The book *Teaching About Evolution and the Nature of Science* presents this alleged dinosaur-bird intermediate as evidence for evolution, saying:

A bird that lived 150 million years ago and had many reptilian characteristics was discovered in 1861 and helped support the hypothesis of evolution proposed by Charles Darwin in *The Origin of Species* two years earlier.[8]

Closer analysis of *Archaeopteryx* shows that it had fully formed flying feathers like those of birds today. Its wings were also elliptical in shape, just like modern woodland birds.[9]

Also like other birds, both its maxilla (upper jaw) and mandible (lower jaw) moved, while in most reptiles, only the mandible moves. *Archaeopteryx's*

Archaeopteryx *is actually an extinct bird.*

brain had a large cerebellum and visual cortex — the same as that found in today's flying birds.[10]

Such scientific findings prompted Alan Feduccia of the University of North Carolina at Chapel Hill (an evolutionist and world authority on birds) to conclude that *Archaeopteryx* is not a reptile at all.[11]

Writing in the journal *Science*, Morell explains:

> Paleontologists have tried to turn *Archaeopteryx* into an earthbound, feathered dinosaur. But it's not. It is a bird, a perching bird. And no amount of "paleobabble" is going to change that.[12]

Another proposed reptile-bird "missing link" was based on the fossil discovery of a creature called *Sinosauropteryx prima*. Initial investigators thought this animal had both feathers and reptile-like features. Their opinion was disproven only about one year later by several leading paleontologists who found that the alleged "feathers" were simply fibers of collagen, the thing from which tendons are made.[13]

A third alleged dinosaur-bird "transition form" was *Mononykus*. It was initially described as a "flightless bird," though feathers were never identified within the fossil.[14]

However, further investigation revealed that:

> Mononykus was clearly not a bird . . . it clearly was a fleet-footed fossorial theropod (a meat-eating dinosaur that dug in the earth with its feet).[15]

Several other reptile-bird or dinosaur-bird transition forms have been suggested. Each one has been disproven, leading Feduccia to conclude:

> It's biophysically impossible to evolve flight from such large bipeds (hind legs) with foreshortened forelimbs and heavy, balancing tails.[16]

It's exactly the wrong anatomy for flight. W.E. Swinton, of British Museum of Natural History in London, likewise concludes:

> There is no fossil evidence of the stages through which the remarkable change from reptile to bird was achieved.[17]

Scientific evidence has yet to show a link between birds and so-called earlier ancestors, the reptiles or dinosaurs. This should not be too surprising. Reptiles and birds are quite different types of creatures. The body of a flying bird is aerodynamically streamlined to decrease wind resistance. Its center of gravity is located in the middle of its wings for balance in flight. A bird has a unique, super-efficient breathing system in which air in the lung flows in only one direction.[18]

It has powerful muscles and distinct long tendons necessary for flight, keen vision, and most distinctly, feathers.

The body of a reptile, on the other hand, lacks the streamlined body features needed for smooth movement through the air. The body weight is more evenly distributed along its head, torso, and tail. Reptiles have a "bellows" type of lung in which air moves in and out along the same passageway. Most powerful muscles are located on the hind legs and pelvis for crawling. Reptiles have uniformly poor vision, and the structural difference between scales and feathers is enormous.[19]

The physical differences separating birds and reptiles are striking. Examining the fossils has yet to reveal any link or evolution that may connect them.

A Horse Is a Horse, of Course!

The background of today's horse is frequently cited as an example of evolution in progress. Many evolutionists explain that the first horse was a dog-sized animal with four toes on the front feet, known as *Hyracotherium (Eohippus)*. It's proposed that this animal evolved to the three-toed *Miohippus*, and finally to the one-toed *Equus* horse of today.

This proposition seems to fit well with the evolutionary concept of gradual change between species. Or does it? First, we have considerable disagreement over whether or not *Hyracotherium* was even a horse at all. Some scientists say that it was actually a primitive rhinoceros, and not related to horses.[20]

Birdsell, an evolutionist himself, describes this popular scheme of horse evolution with the statement:

> Much of this story is incorrect. . . .[21]

Birdsell accurately describes the fossil evidence in the following way. Note that when he use terms like "sudden," "rapid," or "abrupt" differences, he is meaning that no transitional forms have been identified.

> The evolution of the foot mechanism proceeded by rapid and abrupt changes rather than gradual ones. The transition from the form of foot shown by miniature *Eohippus* to larger consistently three-toed *Miohippus* was so abrupt that it even left no record in the fossil deposits. . . . Their foot structure changed very rapidly to a three-toed sprung foot in which the pad disappeared and the two side toes became essentially functionless. Finally, in the Pliocene the line leading to the modern one-toed grazer went through a rapid loss of the two side toes on each foot.[22]

Birdsell is essentially saying that fossils of four-, three-, and then one-toed animals appeared suddenly, without evidence in the fossils of gradual transitions. It is worth noting that no discovery has been made of a possible two-toed horse "transition form" that would help to smooth out the proposed evolution between these animals.

In 1980, 150 evolutionists met at the Chicago Field Museum of Natural History. Boyce Rensberger, reporting on the meeting, stated:

> The popularly told example of horse evolution, suggesting a gradual sequence of changes from four-toed fox-sized creatures

living nearly 50 million years ago to today's much larger one-toed horse, has long been known to be wrong. Instead of gradual change, fossils of each intermediate species appear fully distinct, persist unchanged, and then become extinct. Transitional forms are unknown.[23]

Fossil proof of evolution requires that we discover fossils showing gradual changes from one creature into another. On the other hand, as Rensberger describes above, fossils of each horse-like creature appear fully formed. No detectable changes are noted in their structures. Then, they become extinct and disappear from the fossil record.

Another problem with the popular idea of horse evolution is that the timing does not fit. The theory of evolution says that one species is prone to evolve into another because it is better adapted from survival. In the case of horses, the three-toed form must not have been as hearty as the one-toed, and therefore died out.

However, we know that three-toed and one-toed horses lived together in North America. In Nebraska, for example, a fossil site exists containing five species of horses. A report in the journal *Science* puts it this way:

> The recent discovery of an exquisitely preserved population of primitive *Dinohippus* from Ashfall Fossil Beds in northeastern Nebraska . . . suggests that some individuals were tridactyl (three-toed), whereas others were monodactyl (one-toed).[24]

Evolution demands millions of years for transition to occur between species. The fact that these varieties of horses co-existed is completely inconsistent with evolution's explanation. Add to this the fact that missing links between the types of horses have yet to be found. Rather than lending support for evolution, the history of the horse is more consistent with special creation, that each of these creatures were created separately and at the same time.

What happened regarding horse evolution is actually a good example of evolutionists' over-zealous attempts to make the fossil record "fit" Darwin's theory, when there is actually no support. Though long since thrown out as a hoax, horse evolution still appears in modern high school science books. Consider what other experts have concluded.

French paleontologist and evolutionist Dr. C. Deperet:

The supposed pedigree of the *Equidae* (horses, asses, zebras) is a deceitful delusion, which . . . in no way enlightens us on the paleontological origin of the horse.[25]

Swedish evolutionist, Professor N. Neribert Nilsson, agrees:

The construction of the whole Cenozoic family tree of the horse is a very artificial one, since it was put together from non-equivalent parts, and cannot therefore be a continuous transformation.[26]

Evolutionist Dr. George Gaylor Simpson confirms the hoax as well:

The uniform, continuous transformation of *Hyracotherium* into *Equus,* so dear to the heart of generations of textbook writers, never happened in nature.[27]

WHALE OF A TALE

Whales and dolphins are known by the scientific name *cetacean.* Though they live in water, they are actually mammals. This fact prompted evolutionists to suggest that cetaceans evolved from land mammals, possibly from "a primitive group of hoofed mammals called *Mesonychids.*"[28]

It is important when reading about evolutionary claims to realize the difference between what is actually known from discoveries, and what has been filled in for the sake of a "neat" presentation. Remember what was said earlier about bias? Artists' expressions of what ancient animals actually looked like is often based upon only a few bones, a fraction of the entire skeleton. Writer's "conclusions" frequently are supported by a few facts and much imagination. Such is the case with proposed whale evolution.

Instead, we must minimize our bias and look at the hard evidence. What evidence exists for the idea of a hoofed mammal becoming a whale? *Teaching About Evolution* and *Discover* magazines propose that modern whales evolved via four prior creatures:

- *Mesonychid* (55 million years ago)
- *Ambulocetus* (50 million years ago)
- *Rodhocetus* (46 million years ago)
- *Basilosaurus* (40 million years ago)[29]

The first problem with this proposal is that the time period is far too short. As we discussed in chapter 2, population genetics calculations show that animals with 20 years between each generation (10 years in the case of whales) could pass on no more than about 1,700 mutations in 10 million years.[30]

Almost all mutations are harmful to animals, not helpful. Even if these 1,700 mutations were helpful, this is not nearly enough new genetic code for a land animal to "become" a whale.

A second problem with proposed whale evolution is with the lack of fossils that actually show the transition. The second transitional form, the seven-feet long *Ambulocetus natans* is based upon only a few bones. Examination of the pelvis is especially important. For a land mammal to become a whale it must totally lose its entire pelvis. Yet evolutionary biologist Annalisa Berta points out that we do not have enough of the skeleton to support any connection:

> Since the pelvic girdle is not preserved, there is no direct evidence in *Ambulocetus* for a connection between the hind limbs and the axial skeleton. This hinders interpretations of locomotion in this animal, since many of the muscles that support and move the hind limb originate on the pelvis.[31]

So little of the actual skeleton of *Ambulocetus* exists that it is impossible to be certain what kind of animal it actually was.

For a third problem with proposed whale evolution, the dating that has been done on *Ambulocetus* shows it to be younger than whales that are clearly identified. This makes *Ambulocetus* even less likely to be a walking ancestor of whales.

Consider also the case for *Basilosaurus* — the fourth and last proposed whale transitional form. This fantastic creature was actually a serpent-like sea mammal roughly 70 feet (21 m) long, ten times longer than *Ambulocetus*. The animal dwelled only in the water, showing no transitional features of land and water mammals. Barbara Stahl, a paleontologist and evolutionist herself, concluded:

> The serpentine form of the body and the peculiar shape of the cheek teeth make it plain that these archaeocetes [like *Basilosaurus*] could not possibly have been the ancestor of modern whales.[32]

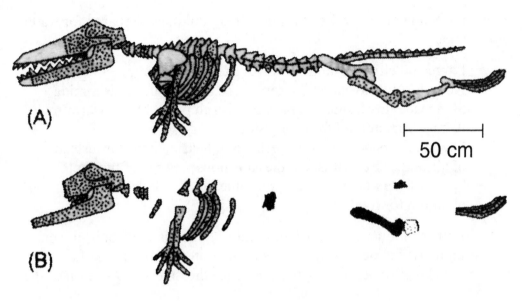

(A) Reconstruction of Ambulocetus, *"at the end of the power stroke during swimming."*[33] *The stippled bones were all that were found, and the shaded ones were found five meters above the rest. (B) With the "additions" removed, there really isn't much left of* Ambulocetus.

Whale expert G.A. Mchedlidze also concluded that these proposed whale transition forms cannot be defended. Rather, it is more appropriate to consider them completely different animals.[34]

The lack of transitional forms in the fossil record was also confirmed by evolutionary whale expert E.J. Slijper:

> We do not possess a single fossil of the transitional forms between the aforementioned land animals [i.e., carnivores and ungulates] and the whales.[35]

> Most embarrassing to evolutionists is the fact that coelacanth, another whale "missing link"—was caught off the coast of Madagascar in 1938! Coelacanth allegedly disappeared seventy million years ago according to evolutionary theory, and was replaced by more developed species![36]

Is there a link between whales and land mammals? Consider these facts. Compared to any other animals on earth, whales are extremely unique creatures. Some of the traits that make them uniquely prepared for water life include:

- Large and efficient lungs for dives as long as 30 minutes
- Nostrils (blowholes) on the top of the head to aid in swimming
- Skin made up of unusual, fatty blubber to protect body warmth
- A huge, forceful tail for propulsion through water
- Eyes and ears perfected for seeing and hearing in water instead of air, and able to withstand the enormous pressure of the depths
- Special filters in the mouth of some whales (baleen) to filter plankton for food

Another unique trait of whales and dolphins is their built-in sonar. These animals can locate tiny objects in the water from great distances by making clicking sounds and then listening for the time and direction of the echo.[37]

But for this system to work, cetaceans must be able to focus the clicking sound in a particular direction.

We now know that this is the purpose of the small lump, or "melon," on the head of whales and dolphins. This melon is constructed from special fats (lipids) arranged in just the right shape and order. As sound is created by the animal, it travels through the melon, and then exits as a focused beam.[38]

Evolution says that random mutations happened, creating slightly better and slightly worse adapted plants and animals. Those which were better adapted survived longer and reproduced. Their offspring in turn mutated, and so the process continued until entirely new species emerged.

Yet whales and dolphins are strikingly different from any other living thing. For them to have evolved via random mutations — putting just the right lipid, blubber, filter, sound sensor, blowhole, and tail muscle in just the right place — is mathematically so unlikely as to be absurd. What's more, gradual step-by-step evolution of these organs must overcome another huge obstacle: They are almost useless until fully formed.

A dolphin with a small, malformed melon on its forehead has no advantage over a dolphin without one. A whale with slightly thicker skin will become just as cold as one with normal skin. One whose eyes can withstand water pressure to a depth of 30 feet has no great advantage of one that can only dive to 20 feet.

For natural selection to have "worked," even the smallest of mutations or developments must lead to a "superior" creature. Otherwise, there would be nothing to make that creature more likely to out-live the others. Yet partial developments like half a wing, a fused toe, or a little fat on the forehead offer nothing superior to the animal. In fact, the "evolutionary step" may well make the creature more likely *not* to survive!

THE CLOCK IS WAY OFF!

Many scientists agree that the fossil record does not show evidence of gradual change from one animal or plant into another. Another challenge to evolution centers around the geologic column, sometimes also known as the geologic clock. Uniformitarianism (a concept that things remain steady) says that the deeper we dig down into the earth, the older are the objects we'll find. If evolution is correct, then the layer of oldest fossils — called the Cambrian layer — should be buried deepest. It just makes sense. But what does the geologic column actually reveal?

Often, fossil layers of the geologic column are completely out of order. Evolutionists, for example, identify trilobites as the very earliest life forms, the most "primitive" known creatures. Yet on June 1, 1968, William Meister, found the fossils of several trilobites in Utah in what appeared to be the fossilized, sandaled footprint of a man![39]

Dr. Clifford Burdick, another geologist, found more evidence that men and trilobites did live together when he discovered the footprints of a barefoot child, one of which contained a compressed trilobite![40]

But wait. There's still more confusion within the geologic column. Manmade artifacts have been discovered in solid rock strata (layers) that some claim were laid over billions of years ago: a thimble, bell, gold chain, spoon, metal vase, screw, nails, coin, and a doll. In one particularly remarkable find, a modern iron hammer was discovered embedded in stone near London, Texas. Geologists computed the rock layer to be four hundred million years old! If the rock was really this old, how can we account for these objects also being there?

Dr. Walter Lammerts describes the problem like this:

> The actual percentage of areas showing this progressive order from the simple to the complex is surprisingly small. Indeed, formations with very complex forms of life are often found resting directly on the basic granites. Furthermore, I have in my own files a list of over 500 cases that attest to a reverse order, that is, simple forms of life resting on top of more advanced types.[41]

The geologic column simply does not show evidence of either transitional forms or less-complex to more-complex creatures. Yet illustrations such as these are frequent in our school textbooks.

The geologic column is a clever "picture" that diametrically illustrates the proposed theory of evolutionary history. Though presented in modern biology and geology textbooks as proven fact, the fossil record proves decisively otherwise.

Evolutionist Dr. Colin Patterson, the owner and proprietor of the most complete fossil collection in the world, regarding fossil evidence for evolution, says:

> There is not one single transitional form in the fossil record for which we could make a water tight argument.[42]

Ronald R. West, Ph.D, assistant professor of paleobiology at Kansas State University, regards the fossil evidence as equally unconvincing:

> Contrary to what most scientists write, the fossil record does not support the Darwinian theory of evolution.[43]

ON WITH THE SHOW

Enough about speculation. Enough about evolutionists predicting what the geologic column will reveal. Instead, what does it actually show? As scientists continue the search, the same evidence is found over and over again, regardless of where they dig. The fossils show that all known forms of life appeared at the same time! They are not laid down in layers, with the most primitive on the bottom. Rather, they were all found present at once. *Time* magazine describes the Cambrian period fossils (the very oldest fossils) like this:

> In a bust of creativity like nothing before or since, nature appears to have sketched out the blueprints for virtually the whole of the animal kingdom.[44]

The lower four-fifths of the earth's crust shows no sign of life. Then, suddenly, life abruptly appears out of nowhere! Just as if it were all created at once. More than 5,000 species are found in the Cambrian layers, with no evidence of transitional forms and with no evidence of evolution. What's more, these fossils demonstrate modern, fully formed creatures! The Cambrian layers have complete jellyfish, trilobites (with eyes as complex as vertebrate eyes), urchins, sponges, and a host of other perfectly formed invertebrates.

Time's report continues:

> Since 1987, discoveries of major fossil beds in Greenland, in China, in Siberia, and now in Namibia have shown that the period of biological innovation occurred at virtually the same instant in geologic time all around the world. What could possibly have powered such a radical advance?

Stephen J. Gould, one of the best-noted evolutionists, has the same interpretation regarding the fossil record:

> New species almost always appeared suddenly in the fossil record with no intermediate links to ancestors in older rocks of the same region.[45]

Another top evolutionist, G.G. Simpson, came to the same conclusion as Gould:

> It remains true, as every paleontologist knows, that most new species, genera, and families . . . appear in the record suddenly and are not led up to by known, gradual, completely continuous, transitional sequences.[46]

This problem even frustrated Darwin. He wrote in *Origin*:

> The abrupt manner in which whole groups of species suddenly appear in certain formations has been urged by several paleontologists . . . as a fatal objection to the belief in the transmutation of species. If numerous species, belonging to the same genera of families, have really started into life at once, the fact would be fatal to the theory of evolution through natural selection.[47]

No transitional forms. No gradually more complex living creatures. Just all modern plants and animals, appearing at the same time, everywhere.

HAD ENOUGH OF HARD ROCK?

Scientists have studied literally billions of fossils of ancient invertebrates and many fossils of ancient fish. The evolution of invertebrates into vertebrates (such as fish) is believed to have required many millions of years.

It seems obvious then, that if we find fossils of the invertebrates and fossils of the fish, we surely ought to find the fossils of the transitional forms between them.

Similarly, we have fossils of crossopterygian fishes which evolutionists claim transformed into amphibians. Since evolution from fish to amphibians should have required many millions of years (during which millions, even billions, of the transitional forms must have lived) many of these transitional forms should be fossilized. Yet, none have been found.

No transitional forms have been clearly identified. But it is also true that not all the fossils on earth have been examined. Could it be that we simply have not looked long enough or deep enough? By any account, over the last 150 years we have examined a good selection of the fossils that exist. Best estimation has it that our museums contain about 250,000 different kinds of fossilized species, and that these represent billions of studied fossils.

We can speculate about the contents of unstudied fossils. Yet scientists believe we have indeed examined enough fossils to draw conclusions about those yet to be found. George summed up the state of affairs:

> There is no need to apologize any longer for the poverty of the fossil record. In some ways it has become almost unimaginably rich and discovery is outpacing integration.[48]

Sampling of the fossils has now been so thorough that it's unreasonable to blame the lack of transitional forms on insufficient research. After 150 years of intense searching, a large number of obvious transitional forms would surely have been discovered if they ever did exist.

GEOLOGIC

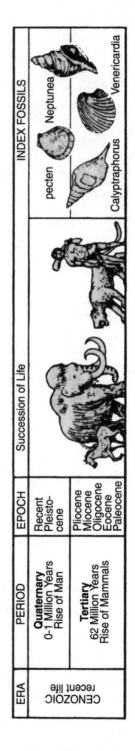

ERA	PERIOD	EPOCH
CENOZOIC recent life	**Quaternary** 0–1 Million Years Rise of Man	Recent Pleisto-cene
	Tertiary 62 Million Years Rise of Mammals	Pliocene Miocene Oligocene Eocene Paleocene

INDEX FOSSILS — Neptunea, pecten, Venericardia, Calyptraphorus

Succession of Life

TIME SCALE

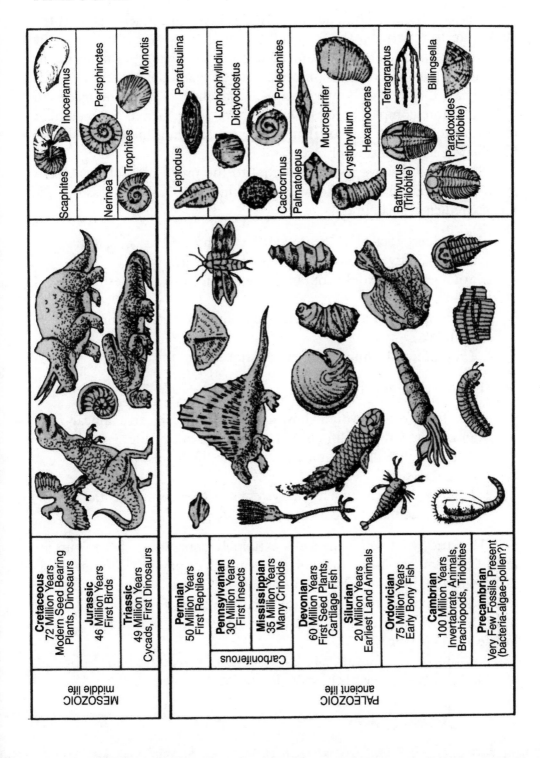

ERA	PERIOD
MESOZOIC middle life	**Cretaceous** 72 Million Years Modern Seed Bearing Plants, Dinosaurs
	Jurassic 46 Million Years First Birds
	Triassic 49 Million Years Cycads, First Dinosaurs
PALEOZOIC ancient life	**Permian** 50 Million Years First Reptiles
	Pennsylvanian 30 Million Years First Insects (Carboniferous)
	Mississippian 35 Million Years Many Crinoids (Carboniferous)
	Devonian 60 Million Years First Seed Plants, Cartilage Fish
	Silurian 20 Million Years Earliest Land Animals
	Ordovician 75 Million Years Early Bony Fish
	Cambrian 100 Million Years Invertebrate Animals, Brachiopods, Trilobites
	Precambrian Very Few Fossils Present (bacteria-algae-pollen?)

Fossil labels: Inoceramus, Scaphites, Perisphinctes, Nerinea, Trophites, Monotis, Leptodus, Parafusulina, Lophophyllidium, Dictyoclostus, Cactocrinus, Prolecanites, Palmatolepus, Mucrospirifer, Crystiphyllium, Hexamoceras, Bathyurus (Trilobite), Tetragraptus, Billingsella, Paradoxides (Trilobite)

Retro Hard Rock: The Facts Revisited

Between the amoeba and the jellyfish, between the jellyfish and the vertebrate fish, between the frog and the bird, between the cow and the whale, between the chimpanzee and modern man, imagine how many multi-billions of transitional forms (intermediate steps) modern paleontologists should have discovered showing these gradual changes from one species to a higher, more complex species. Darwin himself predicted, "The number of intermediate and transitional links between all living and extinct species must have been inconceivably great."

Such fossil discoveries are essential to the proof of evolution. Let's review again just what evidence we are looking for among the fossils. Evolution predicts we will find:

1. The oldest rocks that bear evidence of life would contain the most primitive forms of life capable of fossilization.
2. Younger rocks would contain evidence of more complex forms of life.
3. There would be a gradual change in life forms from simple to complex.
4. There would be huge numbers of transitional forms.

The creation model predicts:

1. The fossil record would show a sudden and explosive appearance of very diverse and highly complex forms of life.
2. There would not be a gradual change in life forms from simple to complex.
3. There would be a regular and systematic absence of transitional forms since there were no transitional forms.[49]

The study of fossil evidence is extremely demanding, both from an intellectual standpoint and the enormous amount of physical labor involved. Fortunately for us, many respectable scientists have invested years studying fossils and looking for such evidence. What have they found? Recent statements by the world's leading evolutionists reveal the overall verdict as told by the fossil evidence.

Dr. Stephen J. Gould, professor of geology and paleontology at Harvard University, reveals his position in these quotes:

All paleontologists know that the fossil record contains precious little in the way of intermediate forms; transitions between major groups are characteristically abrupt.[50]

The absence of fossil evidence for intermediary stages between major transitions in organic design, indeed our inability, even in our imagination, to construct functional intermediates in many cases, has been a persistent and nagging problem for gradualistic accounts of evolution.[51]

The extreme rarity of transitional forms in the fossil record persists as the trade secret of paleontology. The evolutionary trees that adorn our textbooks have data only at the tips and nodes of their branches: the rest is inference however reasonable, not the evidence of the fossils . . . yet to preserve our favored account of evolution by natural selection we view our data as so bad that we never see the very process we profess to study.[52]

The sincere conclusions of other leaders in evolution are further revealed in this personal letter from Dr. Colin Patterson, senior paleontologist at the British Museum of National History, London:

I fully agree with your comments on the lack of direct illustration of evolutionary transitions in my book (*Evolution*). If I knew of any, fossil or living, I would have certainly have included them. . . . Yet Gould and the American Museum people are hard to contradict when they say there are no transitional fossils. . . . I will lay it on the line — there is not one such fossil for which one could make a watertight argument.[53]

Dr. D.V. Ager, president of the British Geological Association further sums up the lack of fossil evidence:

It must be significant that nearly all the evolutionary stories I learned as a student . . . have now been debunked. . . . The point emerges that, if we examine the fossil record in detail, whether at the level of orders or of species, we find — over and over again — not gradual evolution, but the sudden explosion of one group at the expense of another.[54]

Paleontologist Stephen Stanley of Johns Hopkins University also describes the disappointing results of his search for evidence of evolution. He says, in essence, "there are no transition forms, no gradual changes":

> The known fossil record fails to document a single example of phyletic evolution accomplishing a major morphologic transition, and hence offers no evidence that the gradualistic model can be valid.[55]

Dr. Mark Ridley, Oxford zoologist, describes the evolutionists' recent mass exodus from using the fossil record as proof of evolution:

> In any case, no real evolutionist, whether gradualist or punctuationist, uses the fossil record as evidence in favor of the theory of evolution as opposed to special creation.[56]

What paleontology says regarding the fossil record and what is still being taught in textbooks are on the same highway traveling in exactly opposite directions. Although the "family tree" showing evolution from single-celled creatures up to humans continues to be presented in most high school and college textbooks as accepted scientific fact, many honest and empirical scientists flatly deny its validity. What's more, the lack of finding any fossil evidence for evolution is not a new conclusion. As early as the 1930s and 1940s, leaders in paleontology realized the deficiency.

Consider the conclusions of the world's foremost evolutionary paleontologist, George Gaylord Simpson. In his book *Tempo and Mode in Evolution*, he states that nowhere has there been found any trace of a fossil that can be identified as a transitional form:

> This regular absence of transitional forms is not confined to mammals, but is an almost universal phenomenon, as has long been noted by paleontologists. It is true of almost all orders of all classes of animals, both vertebrate and invertebrate. Absolutely, it is also true of the classes, and of the major animal phyla, and it is apparently also true of analogous categories of plants.[57]

Regarding the fossils of major groups of living things, Clark writes, "No matter how far back we go in the fossil record of previous animal life upon earth, we find no trace of any animal forms which are intermediate between the various major groups or phyla." And later he continues: "Since we have not the slightest evidence, either among the living or the fossil ani-mals, of any intergrading types following the major groups, it is a fair sup-position that there never have been any such intergrading types."[58]

Dr. D.B. Kitts explains the difference between the fantasy and the fact:

> Despite the bright promise that paleontology provides a means of "seeing" evolution, it has presented some nasty difficul-ties for evolutionists, the most notorious of which is the presence of "gaps" in the fossil record. Evolution requires intermediate forms between species and paleontology does not provide them.[59]

The absence of transitional forms (missing links) in the fossil record continues to plague scientists in search of evolution. Darwin himself was aware of the lack of fossil evidence for evolution, and questioned his own theory. Consider his statement in *The Origin of Species*:

> Why then is not every geological formation and every stratum full of such intermediate links? Geology assuredly does not reveal any such finely graduated organic chain; and this, perhaps, is the most obvious and serious objection which can be urged against the theory.[60]

The conclusions made by these scientists are not exceptions. Rather, they illustrate what most credible specialists have well documented: the absence of transitional forms between "types." While variations among plants and animals are occasionally seen within the same species, the ab-sence of transitional forms between species is consistent and systematic.

Summing Up

Proof of evolution requires that we find fossils of transitional forms, that is, fossils of species in the process of evolving into new species. To evolve from a bacteria to a plant, a reptile to a bird, a cow to a whale, or from an ape to a man would require trillions on trillions of such intermedi-ate steps. Although the earth's crust is a vast museum of trillions of fossils, NO such transitional forms or "missing links" have been found. The "fossil record" gives no support for the theory of evolution. What do the fossils actually show? They demonstrate the sudden, simultaneous appearance of modern, fully formed creatures of all varieties — just what we'd expect to find if life was indeed created all at once.

ENDNOTES

1 Pierre-Paul Grassé, *Evolution of Living Organisms* (New York, NY: Academic Press, 1977), p. 4.

2 D.J. Futuyma, *Science on Trial* (New York, NY: Pantheon Books, 1983), p. 197.

3 D.B. Wilson, editor, *Did the Devil Make Darwin Do It?* "Interpreting Earth History," by B.F. Glenister and B.J. Witzke (Ames, IA: Iowa State University Press, 1983), p. 58.

4 N.F. Hughes, *Paleobiology of Angiosperm Origins: Problems of Mesozoic Seed-Plant Evolution* (Cambridge, MA: Cambridge University Press, 1976), p. 1–2.

5 C.B. Beck, *Origin and Early Evolution of Angiosperms* (New York, NY: Columbia University Press, 1976).

6 C.A. Arnold, *An Introduction to Paleobotany* (New York, NY: McGraw-Hill Publishing Company, 1947), p. 7.

7 A.M. MacLeod and L.S. Cobley, editors, *Contemporary Botanical Thought* (Chicago, IL: Quadrangle Books, 1961), p. 97, quoting E.J.H. Corner.

8 National Academy of Science, *Teaching about Evolution and the Nature of Science* (Washington, DC: National Academy Press, 1998), p. 8.

9 A. Feduccia, "Evidence from Claw Geometry Indicating Arboreal Habits of *Archaeopteryx*," *Science*, 259(5096):790-793 (February 5, 1993).

10 D. Menton and C. Wieland, "Bird Evolution Flies Out the Window," *Creation Ex Nihilo*, 16(4):16-19 (September–November 1994).

11 A. Feduccia, "Evidence from Claw Geometry Indicating Arboreal Habits of *Archaeopteryx*," *Science*, 259(5096):790-793 (February 5, 1993).

12 V. Morell, "*Archaeopteryx*, Early Bird Catches a Can of Worms," *Science*, 259(5096):764-65 (February 5, 1993).

13 *New Scientist*, 154(2077):13 (April 12, 1997)
    Creation, 19(3):6 (June-August 1997).

14 A. Perle et. al., "Flightless Bird from the Cretaceous of Mongolia," *Nature*, 362:623-626 (1993); note correction of the name to *Mononykus*, as Perle et. al.'s choice, *Mononychus*, was already taken, *Nature*, 363:188 (1993).

15 J.H. Ostrom, D.P. Prothero, and R.M. Schoch, editors, *Major Features of Vertebrate Evolution*, "On the Origin of Birds and of Avian Flight," edited by D.P. Prothero and R.M. Schoch (Knoxville, TN: University of Tennessee Press, 1994), p. 160–177.

16 A. Gibbons, "New Feathered Fossil Brings Dinosaurs and Birds Closer," *Science*, 274:720-721 (1996).

17 A.J. Marshall, editor, *Biology and Comparative Physiology of Birds*, "The Origin of Birds" (chapter 1), by W.E. Swinton (New York, NY: Academic Press, 1960), Vol. 1, p. 1.

18 Michael Denton, *Evolution: A Theory in Crisis* (Bethesda, MD: Adler & Adler, 1985), p. 199–213.
    K. Schmidt-Nielsen, "How Birds Breathe," *Scientific American* (December 1971): p. 72–79.

19 A.H. Brush, "On the Origin of Feathers," *Journal of Evolutionary Biology*, 9:131-142 (1996).

20 G.A. Kerkut, *Implications of Evolution* (New York, NY: Pergamon Press, 1960), p. 149.

21 J.B. Birdsell, *Human Evolution* (Chicago, IL: Rand McNally College Pub. Co., 1975), p. 169.

22 Ibid., p. 170.

23 Boyce Rensberger, *Houston Chronicle* (November 5, 1980), sec. 4, p. 15.

24 B.J. Macfadden, *Fossil Horses* (Cambridge, MA: Cambridge University Press, 1992), p. 255.

25 C. Deperet, *Transformation of the Animal World* (New York, NY: Arno Press, 1980), p. 105.

26 N. Nilsson, *Synthetische Artbuilding* (Lund, Sweden: Verlag CWE Gleerup, 1954).

27 G. Simpson, *Life of the Past* (New Haven, CT: Yale University Press, 1953), p. 125, 127.

28 *Teaching About Evolution and the Nature of Science* (National Academy of Science, 1998), p. 18.

29 National Academy of Science, *Teaching About Evolution and the Nature of Science*, p. 18.
    C. Zimmer, "Back to the Sea," *Discover* (January 1995): p. 83.

30 W.J. ReMine, *The Biotic Message* (St. Paul, MN: St. Paul Science, 1993), chapter 8.

31 J.G.W. Thewissen, S.T. Hussain, and M. Arif, "Fossil Evidence for the Origin of Aquatic Loco-
     motion in Archeocete Whales," *Science*, 263(5144):210–212 (January 14, 1994). Perspective by
     A. Berta, "What is a Whale?" same issue, p. 180–181.

32 B.J. Stahl, *Vertebrate History: Problems in Evolution* (New York, NY: McGraw-Hill, 1974), p.
     489.

33 Ibid.

34 G.A. Mchedlidze, *General Features of the Paleobiological Evolution of Cetacea* (Rotterdam: A.A.
     Balkema, 1986), p. 91, translated from Russian.

35 E.J. Slijper, *Dolphins and Whales* (Ann Arbor, MI: University of Michigan Press, 1962), p. 17.

36 Michael Pitman, *Adam and Evolution* (London: Rider, 1984), p. 235–236.

37 R. Howlett, "Flipper's Secret," *New Scientist*, 154(2088):34-39 (June 28, 1997).

38 U. Varanasi, H.R. Feldman, D.C. Malins, "Molecular Basis for Formation of Lipid Sound
     Lens in Echolocating Cetaceans," *Nature*, 255(5506): 340–343, (May 22, 1975).

39 W.A. Criswell, *Did Man Just Happen?* (Grand Rapids, MI: Zondervan Pub. House, 1973), p.
     120.

40 A.E. Wildersmith, *The Natural Sciences Know Nothing of Evolution* (Green Forest, AR: Master
     Books, Inc., 1981), p. 166.

41 Wayne Jackson, *The Mythology of Modern Geology* (Stockton, CA: Apologetics Press, 1980), p.
     15, quoting Walter Lammerts, "Growing Doubts: Is Evolution Theory Valid?" *Christianity To-
     day*, vol. 6 (September 14, 1962): p.4.

42 *The Bible-Science Newsletter* (August 1981).

43 Ronald R. West, "Paleoecology and Uniformitarianism," *Compass*, vol. 45 (May 1968): p. 216.

44 J. Madeleine Nash, "When Life Exploded," *Time* (December 1995): p. 68.

45 D.M. Raup, *Field Museum of Natural History Bull*, vol. 50 (1979): p. 22.

46 T.N. George, *Science Progress*, vol. 48 (1960): p. 1.

47 Charles Darwin, *The Origin of Species* (London: J.M. Dent & Sons Ltd., 1971), p. 344.

48 T.N. George, *Science Progress*, 48:1 (1960).

49 Bert Thompson, *Biological Evolution* (Montgomery, AL: Apologetics Press, Inc.), p. 16–17.

50 S.J. Gould, "The Return of Hopeful Monsters," *Natural History*, vol. 86 (6) (June–July 1977): p.
     24.

51 S.J. Gould, "Is a New and General Theory of Evolution Emerging?" *Paleobiology*, vol. 6(1)
     (January 1980): p. 127.

52 Gould, "The Return of Hopeful Monsters," p. 22.
         S.J. Gould, "Evolution's Erratic Pace," *Natural History*, vol. 86(5) (May 1977): p. 14

53 Luther D. Sunderland, *Darwin's Enigma* (San Diego, CA: Master Books, 1984), p. 89, quoting a
     personal letter (written April 10, 1979) from Dr. Colin Patterson to Luther D. Sunderland.

54 "The Nature of the Fossil Record," *Proceedings of the Geological Association*, vol. 87, no. 2
     (1976): p. 132–133.

55 Stephen Stanley, *Macroevolution: Pattern and Process* (1979), p. 39.

56 "Who Doubts Evolution?" *New Scientist*, vol. 90 (June 25, 1981): p. 831.

57 George G. Simpson, *Tempo and Mode in Evolution* (New York, NY: Columbia University Press,
     1944), p. 107.

58 A.H. Clark, *The New Evolution: Zoogenesis* (Baltimore, MD: Williams and Wilkins, 1930), p.
     189, 196.

59 D.B. Kitts, "Paleontology and Evolutionary Theory," *Evolution*, vol. 28 (Sept. 1974): p. 467.

60 Charles Darwin, *The Origin of Species* (London: J.M. Dent & Sons Ltd., 1971), p. 292–293,
     chapter 10, "On the Imperfection of the Geological Record."

CHAPTER 5

HUMAN EVOLUTION? NOT!

Uniquely Human

Humans are very unique creatures. Contrasted from animals, human learning, reasoning, and communication abilities are completely unmatched. Yet humans also possess some physical similarities with other primates, such as an opposing thumb and the ability to walk upright. Though the intellectual differences are great, and there are still many physical contrasts, it's commonly taught that humans evolved from apes via several ape-like ancestors. What kind of proof exists for this view?

First let's consider the fossils of so-called ape-human transitional forms. It is frequently proposed by evolutionists that modern humans evolved from apes through the following new species, or missing links:

> *Ramapithecus*
> *Australopithecus*
> *Homo habilis*
> *Homo erectus* (Java man, Peking man)
> *Homo sapiens* (modern man)[1]

Trying to sort out whether or not a fossilized skeleton is related to *Homo sapiens* (human beings) can be a challenging undertaking. Consider just three of the factors that must be considered:

- **Features of the fossils.** In the process of analyzing fossils, scientists look at many features, comparing them with what is known about modern apes, modern man, and other similar fossils. Specifically, scientists pay attention to the size and shape of the skull, the form

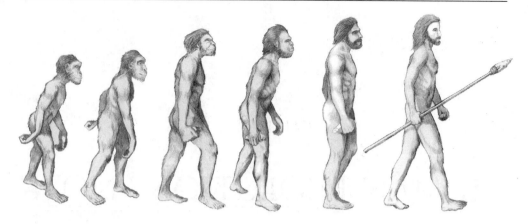

The proposed evolution of man.

of the brow ridges above the eyes, and the way the cheek bones are swept back relative to the jaw. They also pay attention to the length and shape of teeth, jaw configuration, length and shape of arms and legs, slant of the pelvis and lower back, form of the feet, and volume of the cranium — which suggests the size of the creature's brain.

Few skeletons are completely intact. In fact, often the only remains found are pieces of skull, pelvis, and scattered extremities. This makes the task of proving just what they are even more difficult.

- **Number of similar fossils.** Another challenge is the fact that so few suspected ape-human transitional forms have been discovered. The dinosaur supposedly lived 220 million years ago. Tens of thousands of near-perfect dinosaur fossils have been found on all seven continents. Man has been around supposedly for at least the last million years. Why are there so few fossils even remotely thought to be from these "ape-men"? The total number of hominid (ape-men) fossils ever found on earth wouldn't fill the top of a standard size billiard table. The small number of fossils makes a strong case for evolution considerably more difficult.

- **Age of the fossils.** Not only is the form of the fossil important, but so is the age assigned to it. If we are trying to prove, for example, that Animal A evolved into Animal B, dating methods should show that Animal A is indeed older than B. Assigning proper dates to proposed human ancestors is, however, filled with disagreement even among evolutionists themselves.

RAMAPITHECUS

Fossil material given the name *Ramapithecus* was first discovered in 1932 in northwestern India by a Yale graduate student. Similar fossilized remains were also found in Kenya, Europe, and Yunnan Province of China. Initially, *Ramapithecus* was declared to be a branch on the evolutionary tree leading to humans. But this conclusion was based only on similarities between a few *Ramapithecus* teeth and jaw fragments, and those of modern humans. Challenges to the idea lay just ahead.

Ramapithecus

Humans are known by the term *Homo sapiens*. It's helpful to know that the term "homo" or "hominid" is frequently used to identify species thought to be human-like. One researcher who studied *Ramapithecus,* Dr. Roberty Eckhardt of the anthropology department at Pennsylvania State University, sums up the findings of his and many others regarding *Ramapithecus* and other supposed human ancestors:

> Neither is there compelling evidence for the existence of any distinct hominid species during this interval, unless the designation "hominid" means simply any individual ape that happens to have small teeth and a corresponding small face.[2]

Like Dr. Eckhardt, the following is a list of just some of the scientists (mostly in the evolutionary persuasion) who have documented their abandonment of the claim that *Ramapithecus* is a link between ape and man.

Richard Leakey and Roger Leewin
W.C.O. Hill
David Pilbeam
Peter Andrews
Allen L. Hammon
Andrienne L. Zihlman
Leonard D. Greenfield

Today, most evolutionists classify *Ramapithecus* as an extinct ape. It is just one of a long series of creatures that were initially suggested as missing links. But when more complete evidence was examined, the creature was definitely relegated to the ape family.

AUSTRALOPITHECUS IS NOT AMONG US

The next creature, chronologically speaking, said to be a human ancestor is *Australopithecus*. Evolutionists variously claim it lived 1 to 4.5 million years ago. The first fossil was discovered in 1924 by Raymond Dart, who drew attention to the ape-like features of the skull, but thought the teeth were more human-like.[3]

Other creatures were also identified and given names reflecting their similarity:

Australopithecus

Australopithecus africanus
Australopithecus robustus
Australopithecus afarensis

All these animals had small brains, taking up about 500 cc or less of space, about one-third the space occupied by human brains. They also had large, ape-like jaws, with cheek teeth similar to modern gorillas. Unfortunately, only a few fragments of pelvis, limb, and foot bones were ever recovered of the *Australopithecus* line of creatures.

In 1974 Donald Johanson rocked the world with his claim of discovering several pieces of *Australopithecus* skeletons in Ethiopia, which he alleged were human ancestors. One particular *Australopithecus* was given the name "Lucy." It was three and one-half feet tall, with a brain size of 380 to 450 cc.[4]

The media attention to this find was enormous, and Johanson was famous almost overnight. With time, however, cooler scientific heads prevailed and Lucy was re-examined. Today, many leading scientists (most of them evolutionists themselves) disagree that these bones represent a step in human evolution. Consider what the experts say about Lucy and other australopithecines:

Anatomist Charles Oxnard is one of the best respected experts on this subject. His own analysis of the bones of *Australopithecus africanus* led him to conclude that this creature was very unlike either humans or chimpanzees.[5]

After more research on the entire proposed australopithecines series, Oxnard announced he does not find any of the australopithecines to be related to humans:

> It is now recognized widely that the australopithecines are not structurally closely similar to humans, that they must have been living at least in part in arboreal [tree] environments, and that many of the later specimens were contemporaneous [living at the same time] or almost so with the earlier members of the genus *Homo*.[6]

Notice the last phrase. He is saying that *Australopithecus* was found living with humans. How then, could *Australopithecus* possibly be a human ancestor? More about this later.

Though over-zealously manipulated by earlier evolutionists, further recent study places *Australopithecus* in the ape family, not in the lineage of modern man. Evolutionist and paleontologist, professor Joseph Weiner, agrees:

> The first impression given by all the skulls from the different populations of *Australopithecus* is of a distinctly ape-like creature. . . . The ape-like profile of *Australopithecus* is so pronounced that its outline can be superimposed on that of a female chimpanzee with a remarkable closeness of fit. In this respect and also in the lack of chin and in possession of strong supra-orbital ridges, *Australopithecus* stands in strong contrast to modern (man) *Homo sapiens*."[7]

Sir Solly Zuckerman, secretary of the Zoological Society of London and chief scientist advisor to the British government, screams for integrity among overzealous evolutionists:

> The australopithecine skull is in fact so overwhelmingly simian (ape) as opposed to human that the contrary proposition could be equated to an assertion that black is white.[8]

Richard Leakey, director of National Museum in Kenya, son of the famous paleontologist Louis Leakey, also issues a plea for integrity:

Lucy's skull (*Australopithecus afarensis*) was so incomplete that most of it was imagination, made of plaster of Paris, thus making it impossible to draw any firm conclusion about what species she belonged to.[9]

He further states:

It is overwhelmingly likely that Lucy was no more than a variety of pygmy champanzee. The evidence for the alleged transformation from ape to man is extremely unconvincing.[10]

Fossils of *Australopithecus* have been studied in painstaking detail: their manner of walking, the structure of their ear, pattern of tooth development, their long and powerful forearms, short hindlimbs, structure of their

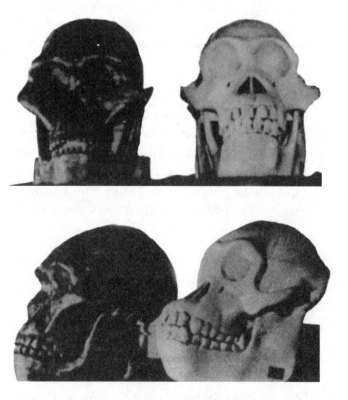

Frontal and diagonal views of Australopithecus africanus *(left) and cast of an orangutan skull (right).*[11]

feet, small-sized brains, and very ape-like skulls, jaws, and faces. These prove that *Australopithecus* was an ape and in no way related to man. Donald Johanson himself, the discoverer of Lucy, later concluded that *Australopithecus africanus* (Lucy) was not related to humans at all![12]

HOMO HABILIS — ANOTHER NOT AMONG US

Homo habilis

Several other claims have been made of fossilized creatures that initially seemed more man-like than was *Australopithecus. Homo habilis* is the name assigned to one such series of fossils. The adults were about three and one-half feet tall, with brains about one-third the size of humans, and long heavily built arms. Confusing the research is the fact that so many fossils of such wide variety have been attributed to *Homo habilis* that it has become known as a "waste basket" designation. After painstaking study, most palentologists today believe *Homo habilis* is not related to humans, but is rather a variety of *Australopithecus* ape, more on the order of a chimpanzee or orangutan.[13]

Another fact confusing the proposed evolution of *Australopithecus* to *Homo habilis* is evidence that they both lived together! The eminent paleontologist Stephen J. Gould of Harvard University sums up the difficulty showing any proof of human evolution regarding *Homo habilis*:

> What has become of our ladder if there are three co-existing lineages of hominids (*Australopithecus africanus, Australopithecus robustus*, and *Homo habilis*), none clearly derived from one another? Moreover, none of the three display any evolutionary trends during their tenure on earth: none became brainier or more erect as they approached the present day.[14]

HOMO ERECTUS FROM JAVA, INDONESIA

Homo erectus is a species of creature proposed to be the link just before modern humans. The two best known are Java Man and Peking Man. The story of Java Man begins in 1887 when a Dutch physician, Eugene Dubois, began searching Indonesia for "missing links." Four years later he came across the top portion of a skull, with a femur found about 50 feet

Pithecanthropus

away. From the skullcap, he imagined what the face might actually have looked like. This, along with the human-like femur, convinced Dubois that the creature was an ancestor to humans. He gave it the name *Pithecanthropus erectus* ("erect ape-man"), popularly known as Java Man.

Dubois' announcement generated both attention and doubt. German zoologists tended to think Java Man was actually an ape, the British considered it human, and the French, something between the two. It was not until 30 years later that Dubois confessed to what else he had discovered at the same site: two skulls of modern humans. This immediately explained the human likeness of the femur. It also assured the scientific community that Java Man was not a missing link at all, but actually a coverup! Ultimately, Dubois himself declared that the Java Man skull was simply a giant gibbon of the ape family.[15]

HOMO ERECTUS FROM PEKING

Peking Man (*Sinanthropus pekinensis*) is another find that was identified as *Homo erectus*. This story starts near Peking (now called Beijing) in the 1920s and 1930s, where a group of skulls, jaws, and teeth were found. Nothing else was left of these creatures. Dr. Davidson Black, a professor of anatomy at Union Medical College in Peking, examined just one tooth, thought it to be human-like, and declared that a new ape-man creature had been discovered. It was given the name *Sinanthropus pekinensis*, popularly known as Peking Man.

Once again, the announcement generated a wave of publicity. Other researchers who studied the findings, however, were not as convinced as Black. Marcellin Boule and H.V. Vallois, both paleontologists, examined the fossils and declared:

> In its totality, the structure of the *Sinanthropus* skull is still very ape-like.[16]

Sinanthropus

They also found that its brain size was still considerably less than human. Boule and Vallois concluded that *Sinanthropus* were actually macaques or baboons that were likely killed and eaten by true humans.

Teilhard de Chardin, writing in *L'Anthropologie,* in 1931 similarly states:

> *Sinanthropus* manifestly resembles the great apes closely.[17]

Another frequently overlooked fact about Peking Man is that the fossils of ten modern human individuals were also found at the same site as the *Sinanthropus* skulls.[18]

This discovery makes us question: How could *Sinanthropus* possibly be an ancestor of humans, when there were obviously humans living at the same time? Dr. Black never addressed the subject.

All the fossils for Peking Man mysteriously disappeared sometime between 1941 and 1945. No one since that time has been successful in recovering the bones. Consequently, analysis of Peking Man today is based solely on descriptions and drawings.

All in all, it appears today that Black had committed himself to the discovery of a new species on the basis of a single tooth, and felt motivated to mold the facts to fit his announcement. At the very least, the identification of *Sinanthropus* as a near-man creature was based upon preconceived ideas, desire for fame, and possibly even outright fraud.

Other fossils discovered have also been classified as *Homo erectus*. At present, however, considerable disagreement exists between paleoanthropologists about just which fossils should be classified as *Australopithecus, Homo erectus*, or true humans. Some paleoanthropologists (almost all of whom support evolution) now even classify all *Homo erectus* as true humans and not transitional forms at all.[19]

Challenging to supporters of evolution are not only the features of these skeletons, but the fact that some fossils of true humans have been dated as older than those of *Homo erectus*, from whom humans are supposed to have evolved. Yet that fact is totally inconsistent with evolution. Dr. Duane T. Gish sums up the findings of many researchers:

> At this time, it is our opinion that some specimens attributed to *Homo erectus*, such as Java Man and Peking Man, are definitely from the ape family with no link of any kind to man.[20]

WHAT ABOUT NEANDERTHAL MAN?

First discovered in a cave near Dusseldorf, Germany, Neanderthal Man is one of the most popularized "prehuman" creatures. It is usually portrayed as a semi-erect figure, carrying a club and with a brutish expression. In the one hundred years since found, we now know that Neanderthal Man suffered from the disease known as rickets. Caused by vitamin D deficiency, rickets leaves bones unusually soft and easily malformed. This explains the often ruddy appearance attributed to the Neanderthals.

Recent DNA evidence indicates that Neanderthal was fully human. Analysis made of the DNA within a Neanderthal skeleton was found to be markedly similar to that of modern humans, even when accounting for the fact that it was thousands of years old.[21]

Neanderthalensis

Today we also know that Neanderthal Man stood fully upright, and that in the ab-

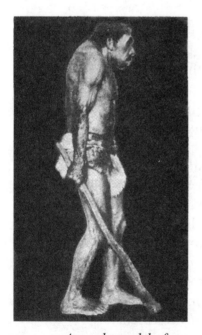

An early model of Neanderthal Man no longer considered valid. (Courtesy of the Department of Library Services, American Museum of Natural History.)

A modern-day model of Neanderthal Man. (Courtesy of the Department of Library Services, American Museum of Natural History.)

sence of disease, its features are no different than modern humans.[22] If a Neanderthal were dressed in jeans and a T-shirt, and went to a ball game, you and I would probably not even notice him or her.

DECEPTION: NEBRASKA MAN

In 1922 a simple tooth was discovered in western Nebraska. After examination, renowned paleontologist Henry Fairfile Osborn announced that the tooth belonged to yet another ape-man ancestor; this one named *Hesperopithecus*, publically known as Nebraska Man. Widely published as a missing link, it was used as pro-evolution evidence in the famous "monkey trial" in Dayton, Tennessee.

Hesperopithecus

Within five years other studies were carried out by authorities who declared that the tooth from Nebraska Man was actually that of a species of wild pig extinct in North America, and now living only in Paraguay.[23]

There was no other evidence of Nebraska Man even left to consider!

FRAUD: PILTDOWN MAN

Another blow to the credibility of searching for human ancestors occurred in 1912. Arthur Smith Woodward, director of the Natural History Museum of London, and Charles Dawson, a medical doctor, declared their discovery of a jaw and part of a skull. Uncovered in a gravel pit near Piltdown, England, the jaw seemed very ape-like and the skull resembled that of a human. They named the creature *Eoanthropus dawsoni* — or Piltdown Man, and estimated him to be about 500,000 years old. Once again, their announcement generated enormous international attention and praise.

However, by the 1950s a new technique was perfected to identify the age of bones. It was based upon measuring the concentration of fluoride that the bones had absorbed from the surrounding soil. Piltdown

Eoanthropus

Man's jaw was tested and found to contain no fluoride, proving that it was not a fossil at all and was only about a year old! The skull did contain fluoride, enough to date it at about 5,000 years old.

This remarkable discrepancy caused the jaw and skull to be carefully re-examined. Scientists discovered that the bones had been soaked in a special chemical just to make them appear old! Ultimately, the jaw was identified from an orangutan ape which had recently died, and the skull that of a modern human. Piltdown Man was judged a complete sham![24]

Clearly, the haste to prove evolution's expectations at any cost — even deliberate fraud — exposes the bias of many in the scientific community. Anthropologist Jaquetta Hawkes correctly observes:

> Accepting this as inevitable and not necessarily damaging, it still comes as a shock to discover how often preconceived ideas have affected the investigation of human origins.
>
> There is, of course, nothing like a fake for exposing such weaknesses among the experts. For example, to look back over the bold claims and subtle anatomical distinctions made by some of our greatest authorities concerning the recent human skull and modern ape's jaw which together composed "Piltdown Man," rouses either joy or pain, according to one's feelings for the scientists.[25]

Call it "evolution at any cost." Some scientists have demonstrated a striking lack of integrity and scientific discipline. Has the situation improved today? In 1983 a group of experts in Europe announced the discovery of a fossil declared to be the oldest human even found, "Orce Man" from southern Spain. French scientists investigated the claim and declared that Orce Man was actually the skull of a four-month-old donkey![26]

Apparantly the drive to prove evolution — against the opposing fossil evidence — is as stong today as ever before.

LIVING ALL TOGETHER, 24-7

Further confounding efforts to show an evolutionary trend is the fact that fossils indicate that the proposed human missing links all lived together at the same time! Richard Leakey and Alan Walker, for example admit that:

> There is evidence from East Africa for late-surviving small *Australopithecus* individuals that were contemporaneous first with *Homo habilis*, then *Homo erectus*.[27]

If evolution claims they came from one another, surely they could have not all been living together! The australopithecines are thought to have lived between one and four million years ago. Yet human footprints were also found and thought to be 3.5 million years old:

> Make no mistake about it. . . . They are like modern human footprints. If one were left in the sand of a California beach today, and a four-year old were asked what it was, he would instantly say that somebody walked there.[28]

Now, if *Australopithecus, Homo habilis,* and *Homo erectus* existed together, how could one have possibly evolved from another? Equally puzzling: How could any of these be pre-human, when human fossils are found buried even deeper than these proposed ancestors of man? Certainly none of these could have evolved into humans. We can trim *Australopithecus, Homo habilis,* and *Homo erectus* right off the tree of human evolution, and just cut the tree down.

As if this evidence were not enough contradiction against evolution, consider the age of other fossils of modern humans. *Homo sapien* bones were recently found in the Cretaceous stratum — a geologic rock layer in Moab, Utah, thought to be 100 million years old, and far older than the one-million-year maximum age evolutionists assign to modern humans.[29]

Even more remarkable are footprints of modern humans far older than those mentioned above. A.E. Wilder Smith writes:

> Human footprints have been repeatedly discovered in the Upper Carboniferous period (supposedly 250 million years old).[30]

Modern humans living 100–250 million years ago would mean that they were present far earlier than the dinosaurs!

No Bones About It

Dr. Charles E. Oxnard, professor of anatomy and human biology, University of Western Australia, shows the fallacy in announcing proof of evolution before the facts are all in:

> In each case although initial studies suggest that the fossils are similar to humans, study of the complete evidence readily shows that the reality is otherwise.[31]

Many scientists agree that the various proposed "ape-men" do not at all make up a series of evolutionary stages. Rather, some were actually varieties of true humans, such as the Neanderthals. Others were entirely non-humans, like the australopithecines. They were of the ape family.

It is clear that when the claims for human ape-ancestors are investigated, we discover that both humans and apes appear in the fossils as fully formed creatures, without transition forms — just as would be expected if both were created that way from the beginning.

Consider the conclusions of several renowned scientists on this matter. Sir Solly Zuckerman spent his entire career searching out proof for evolution, and finding none. He then exposed the dilemma evolutionists are up against in proving that man evolved:

> No scientist could logically dispute the proposition that man, without having been involved in any act of divine creation, evolved from some ape-like creature in a very short space of time (speaking in geological terms) without leaving any fossil traces of the steps of the transformation. As I have already implied, students of the fossil primates have not been distinguished for caution. . . . The record is so astonishing that it is legitimate to ask whether much science is yet to be found in this field at all.[32]

Zuckerman's honesty is commendable, and voiced also by evolutionist Lyall Watson in *Science Digest*:

> Modern apes, for instance, seem to have sprung out of nowhere. They have no yesterday, no fossil record. And the true origin of modern humans — of upright, naked tool-making, big-brained beings — is, if we are to be honest with ourselves, an equally mysterious matter.[33]

Commenting on books on evolution, Dr. Robert Martin, senior research fellow at the Zoological Society of London, concludes:

> In recent years several authors have written popular books on human origins which were based more on fantasy and subjectivity than on fact and objectivity.[34]

Evolutionist and paleontologist Joseph Weiner sums up the study of human evolution:

It is quite obvious that modern man could not have arisen from any ape, let alone a monkey, at all similar to those of today. . . . It is ridiculous to describe man as a "naked" or any other kind of ape.[35]

In the following statement on human evolution Wolfgang Smith, Ph.D. agrees with Weiner:

On the fundamental level, it becomes a rigorously demonstrable fact that there are no transitional types, and that the so-called missing links are indeed non-existent.[36]

Evolutionist Albert C. Ingalls shows his exasperation with the scientific world's massive cover-up and deception:

If man, or even his ape ancestor, or even the ape ancestor's early mammal ancestor, existed as far back as in the Carboniferous period in any shape, then the whole science of geology is so completely wrong that all geologists will resign their jobs and take up truck driving.[37]

Dr. D.V. Ager, president of the British Geological Association, well surmises the lack of fossil evidence:

It must be significant that nearly all the evolutionary stories I learned as a student have now been debunked. . . . The point emerges that, if we examine the fossil record in detail, whether at the level of orders or of species, we find — over and over again — not gradual evolution, but the sudden explosion of one group at the expense of another.[38]

The fossils once thought to be human ancestors are now known to be only those of extinct apes. You and I must ask ourselves, why is human evolution taught as fact in our textbooks and schools? Why do the great museums still carry plaster of Paris representations of ape-men? Perhaps it is because the only other alternative is to admit that humans, as well as other living things, were simply created.

Summing Up

Human beings are extremely unique in comparison to every other living creature. Evolutionists say, however, that humans descended from apes through a series of transitional forms. For evidence they point to several fossil discoveries that they allege show these transitions.

These fossils are hardly full skeletons, though. Usually they consist of only a fragment of skull, pelvis, or long bone. The most popularized of these so-called ape-men fossils are identified as *Ramapithecus*, *Australopithecus*, *Homo habilis*, and *Homo erectus*. It is now widely recognized that the structures of these creatures are not similar to humans, but rather more on the order of the chimpanzee, orangutan, or gibbon.

Neanderthal Man, whose contrived images are common in textbooks, we know today was actually a modern human who suffered from disease known to cause physical deformities. The thirst to find fossils of an ape-man has also led to fraud and deception, best illustrated by so-called Nebraska Man and Piltdown Man.

Further challenging to the idea of human evolution is evidence showing *Australopithecus*, *Homo habilis*, *Homo erectus*, and modern humans all living together at the same time. But this is impossible if they actually evolved from one another! The truth is they did not, and that no reliable evidence exists for human evolution.

ENDNOTES

1 D.T. Gish, *Evolution: The Fossils Still Say No* (El Cajon, CA: Institute for Creation Research, 1995), p. 227.

2 Robert Eckhardt, *Scientific American*, 226 (1): 94 (1972).

3 Raymond A. Dart, *Nature*, 115:195–199 (1925).

4 Donald Johanson and M.A. Edey, *Lucy, the Beginnings of Mankind* (New York, NY: Simon and Schuster, 1981).

5 C.E. Oxnard, *Nature*, 258:389–395 (1975).

6 C.E. Oxnard, *The Order of Man* (New Haven, CT: Yale University Press, 1984).

7 Joseph Weiner, *The Natural History of Man* (New York, NY: Universe Books, 1971), p. 45–46.

8 Solly Zuckerman, *Beyond the Ivory Tower* (London: Weidenfeld & Nicholson, 1970), p. 78.

9 *The Weekly Australian* (May 7–8, 1983): p. 3.

10 "Lucy — Evolution's Solitary Claim for an Ape/Man: Her Position Is Slipping Away," *Creation Research Society Quarterly*, vol. 22, no. 3 (December 1985): p. 144–145.

11 Illustration from "Rusch's Human Fossils," in *Rock Strata and the Bible Record*, P.A. Zimmerman, editor (St. Louis, MO: Concordia Pub. House, 1970).

12 Donald Johanson and T.D. White, *Science*, 203:321 (1979) 207:1104 (1980).

13 Ian Tattersall, *Evolutionary Anthropology*, 1(1):34–36 (1992).
   S. Hartwig-Scherer and R.D. Martin, *Journal of Human Evolution*, 21:439–449 (1991).

14 S.J. Gould, *Natural History*, 85:30 (1976).

15 Marcellin Boule and H.V. Vallois, *Fossil Men* (New York, NY: Dryden Press, 1957), p. 126.
   Niles Eldredge, *Fossils — The Evolution and Extinction of Species* (New York, NY: Harry N. Abrams, Inc., 1991), p. 56.
   W.S. Howell, *Mankind in the Making* (Garden City, NY: Doubleday, 1967), p. 155–156.

16 Boule and Vallois. *Fossil Men*, p. 136.

17 Teilhard de Chardin, *L'Anthropologie* (Paris, 1931).
18 Patrick O'Connell, *Science of Today and the Problems of Genesis, Book 1* (Hawthorne, CA: Christian Book Club of America, 1969).
19 David L. Phillips, *M.A. Thesis* (Northridge, CA: California State University, January 1991), p. 28.
20 Gish, *Evolution: The Fossils Still Say No*, p. 304.
21 M. Lubenow, "Recovery of Neandertal mtDNA: An Evaluation," *Creation Ex Nihilo Technical Journal*, 12(1):87–97 (1998).
22 F. Ivanhoe, *Nature*, 227:577 (1970).
        E. Trunkaus and W.W. Howells, *Scientific American*, 241(6):118 (1979).
23 W.K. Gregory, *Science*, 66:579 (1927).
24 S.J. Gould, *Natural History*, 88(3): 96 (1979).
25 Jaquetta Hawkes, *Nature*, 204:952 (1964).
26 *Moline (Illinois) Daily Dispatch* (May 14, 1984).
27 R.E.F. Leakey and Alan Walker, *Science*, 207:1103 (1980).
28 Johanson and Edey, *Lucy, the Beginnings of Mankind*, p. 245–252.
29 Wayne Jackson, *The Mythology of Modern Geology* (Stockton, CA: Apologetics Press, 1980), p. 31, quoting F.A. Barnes, *Desert Magazine*, 38:36–39 (February, 1975).
30 Jackson, *The Mythology of Modern Geology*, p. 32, quoting A.E. Wilder Smith, *Man's Origin, Man's Destiny* (Wheaton, IL: Harold Shaw Publishers, 1970), p. 300.
31 Dr. Charles E. Oxnard, *Fossils, Teeth and Sex: New Perspectives on Human Evolution* (Seattle, WA and London: University of Washington Press,1987), p. 227.
32 Sir Solly Zuckerman, *Beyond the Ivory Tower* (London: Weidenfeld & Nicholson, 1970), p. 64.
33 "The Walter People," *Science Digest*, vol. 90, no. 5 (May 1982): p. 44.
34 Dr. Robert Martin, "Man Is Not an Onion," *New Scientist* (August 4, 1977): p. 283, 285.
35 Joseph Weiner, *The Natural History of Man* (New York, NY: Universe Books, 1971), p. 33.
36 Wolfgang Smith, *Teilhardism and the New Religion: A Thorough Analysis of the Teachings of Pierre Teilhard de Chardin* (Rockford, IL: Tan Books and Publishers, Inc., 1988), p. 8.
37 Jackson, *The Mythology of Modern Geology*, p. 32–33, quoting Albert C. Ingalls, "The Carboniferous Mystery," *Scientific American* (CLXII, January 1940): p.14.
38 British Geological Association, "The Nature of the Fossil Record," Dr. D.V. Ager, *Proceedings of the Geological Association*, vol. 87, no. 2 (1976): p. 132–133.

CHAPTER 6

CREATION — IT'S EVERYWHERE!

READY, SET, GO!

How did life begin? How can we explain the living marvels of our world? Where did humans come from? Who is our true ancestor? Each of us has pondered these questions. The most insightful of scientists and philosophers have devoted their lives to finding the answers.

Only two alternatives exist. Either we evolved from dead slime through millions of years of random chemical accidents, or we were intentionally designed and created. There are no other options.

Renowned astronomer Robert Jastrow puts the question in perspective:

> Perhaps the appearance of life on the earth is a miracle. Scientists are reluctant to accept that view, but their choices are limited. Either life was created on the earth by the will of a Being outside the grasp of scientific understanding, or it evolved on our planet spontaneously, through chemical reactions occurring in nonliving matter lying on the surface of the planet.
>
> The first theory places the question of the origin of life beyond the reach of scientific inquiry. It is a statement of *faith* in the power of a Supreme Being not subject to the laws of science. The second theory is also an act of *faith*. The act of *faith* consists in assuming that the scientific view of the origin of life is correct, without having concrete evidence to support that belief (emphasis his).[1]

The case could not be better stated than this! Let's review the second option again. The theory of evolution is based upon four assumptions:

1. **Spontaneous generation**. That life began through the chance encounter of highly complex chemicals. In chapter 2 we reviewed the laws of chemistry and probability which show this is clearly impossible.

2. **Random mutation and natural selection**. That spontaneous mutations caused changes in some creatures, making them more likely to survive. Also in chapter 2, we discovered that mutations are usually lethal, or leave the creature sterile at best. And, natural selection provides no real benefit to the creature until the new feature is fully functional. This completely negates the possibility of natural selection.

3. **Enormous time**. That the earth must have been inhabitable for hundreds of millions of years for random mutation and natural selection to have time to develop humans and other advanced animals. In chapter 3 we found that the commonly used dating methods are flawed at best. Considerable scientific evidence points to a young earth.

4. **Fossil record full of transitional forms**. That, if evolution is indeed true, then over the many millions of years there must have lived vast numbers of transitional creatures. Just as we have discovered many tens of thousands of dinosaur fossils, we should also have discovered many tens of thousands of transitional creatures. Yet in chapters 4 and 5 we saw that there are no fossils of transitional creatures, human or otherwise.

EVOLUTION = SCIENCE FICTION

Science has a long history of rational thought and outstanding discoveries. We can define science like this:

science, noun. 1. A branch of knowledge or study dealing with a body of facts systematically arranged and showing the operation of general laws. 2. Systematic knowledge of the physical or material world gained through observation and experimentation.

Science fiction, by contrast, deals in imagination and fantasy. While entertaining, it does not try to pass itself off as being true. It can be defined like this:

> **science fiction**, noun. A form of fiction that draws imaginatively on scientific knowledge and speculation.

There's a huge difference between science (dealing with facts) and science fiction (dealing with fantasy and fairy tales). If we get them confused with one another, we'll miss out on the truth.

We're all familiar with fairy tales. In the movie *The Swan Princess*, for example, the frog with the outrageous French accent was convinced of one particularly enduring fairy tale: If a frog is kissed by a princess, he will become a prince.

FAIRY TALE:
FROG + PRINCESS'S KISS = PRINCE

After multiple attempts, the frog in the movie finally did receive the princess's kiss. Can you guess what happened? He was still a plain, green frog. Any scientist can tell you that the fairy tale is not true. Have a princess kiss as many frogs as she likes, and they'll still be frogs. It would be foolish to think otherwise.

In the world of science today we have a similar fairy tale being portrayed as the truth: that a frog can indeed become a prince through the process of evolution.

SCIENCE FICTION:
FROG + EVOLUTION = PRINCE

Unlike most science fiction, however, this non-truth is not at all entertaining. To support their position, evolutionists employ a great deal of speculation, occasional fraud, and lastly very little, if any, real evidence.

Yet the subtle "pledge of allegiance" to Darwin and his doctrine has been adhered to by virtually every editing board of America's textbooks of science.

Many of the world's most renowned scientists flatly disagree with Darwin on strictly scientific grounds. In his book *The Bone Peddlers*, William Fix opens the evolutionists' secret tomb. "Scientists at the forefront of inquiry have put the knife to classical Darwinism. They have not gone public with this news, but have kept it in their technical papers and inner counsels."[2]

Dr. Colin Patterson, senior paleontologist at the British Museum of Natural History in London, points out evolution's untruths:

> Darwin's evolutionary explanation of the origins of man has been transformed into a modern myth, to the detriment of science and social progress. . . . The secular myths of evolution have had a damaging effect on scientific research, leading to distortion, to needless controversy, and to the gross misuse of science. . . . I mean the stories, the narratives about change over time. How the dinosaurs became extinct, how the mammals evolved, where man came from. These seem to me to be little more than story-telling.[3]

Albert Fleishman, professor of zoology and comparative anatomy at Erlangen University, Germany, rightly concludes:

> The Darwinian theory of descent has not a single fact to confirm it in the realm of nature. It is not the result of scientific research but purely the product of imagination.[4]

Scientist B. Leith admits what many scientists already realize; that support for evolution is unraveling. He wrote:

> The theory of life that undermined nineteenth-century religion has virtually become a religion itself and in its turn is being threatened by fresh ideas. . . . In the past ten years has emerged a new breed of biologists who are considered scientifically respectable, but who have their doubts about Darwinism.[5]

Pierre-Paul Grassé, of the University of Paris and past president of the French Academy of Science, also comments regarding the lack of evidence for evolution:

The deceit is sometimes unconscious, but not always, since some people, owing to their sectarianism, purposely overlook reality and refuse to acknowledge the inadequacies and the falsity of their beliefs.[6]

Dr. S. Lovtrup is emphatic in his analysis:

I believe that one day the Darwinian myth will be ranked the greatest deceit in the history of science. When this happens, many people will pose the question, "How did this ever happen?"[7]

Some in the scientific community continue to swear allegiance to the theory of evolution. They've tried to erect a water-tight seal around its teaching. But more and more scientists and other community leaders, are analyzing the evidence and defecting from Darwin's evolutionary army.

It's time for this fairy tale to be truly exposed. Evolution is wrong. It is not a fact, but a fraud. Hsu, a well-known geologist at the Geological Institute in Zurich, is emphatic in his declaration:

We have had enough of the Darwinian fallacy. It is time that we cry: "The emperor has no clothes."[8]

CREATION — IT'S EVERYWHERE

Evolution, for all its support among teachers and the press, is a concept without "clothes." The only alternative, and the real truth, is that every creature was specifically designed and created.

Dr. Niles Eldridge, paleontologist and evolutionist, of the American Museum of Natural History, declares the only possible answer:

The only competing explanation for the order we all see in the biological world is the notion of special creation.[9]

Professor Richard Dawkins, an atheist himself, came to the same conclusion:

The more statistically improbable a thing is, the less we can believe that it just happened by blind chance. Superficially, the obvious alternative to chance is an intelligent Designer.[10]

He then expresses this fact with poetic enthusiasm:

> Every painting has a painter.
> Every watch has a watchmaker.
> Every book has a writer.
> Every design has a designer.
> Every computer has a programmer.[11]

Hugh Ross, as astronomer and former research fellow at Cal Tech University, sees a very intelligent designer behind the universe:

> The degree of fine-tuning of the 34 different characteristics of the universe that demand exquisite fine-tuning for physical life, measure at least ten trillion trillion trillion times greater than what the most brilliant and powerful and well-equipped humans can accomplish. Just this one characteristic of the universe suggests that the Creator is at least ten trillion trillion trillion times more intelligent, knowledgeable, creative, and powerful than human beings.[12]

Sir Fred Hoyle, professor of astronomy at Cambridge University, and Chandra Wickramasinghe, professor of astronomy and applied mathematics at University College in Cardiff, also see only one solution to the question of our origins:

> Once we see, however, that the probability of life originating at random is so utterly minuscule as to make it absurd, it becomes sensible to think that the favorable properties of physics, on which life depends, are in every respect deliberate. . . . It is, therefore, almost inevitable that our own measure of intelligence must reflect higher intelligence — even to the limit of God.[13]

Paul Davies, Australian physicist/philosopher is more sanguine in his assessment:

> The temptation to believe that the universe is the product of some sort of design is overwhelming. The belief that there is "something behind it all" is one that I personally share with, I suspect, a majority of physicists.[14]

H.S. Lipson, professor of physics at the University of Manchester, urges:

I think that we must go further than this (natural selection and species evolution) and admit that the only acceptable explanation is creation.[15]

Thomas Huxley was a dedicated atheist. So strong were his evolutionary views that he was called "Darwin's Bulldog." Yet even he acknowledged:

"Creation," in the ordinary sense of the word, is perfectly conceivable. I find no difficulty in conceiving that, at some former period, this universe was not in existence, and that it made its appearance in six days (or instantaneously, if that is preferred), in consequence of the volition of some preexisting Being.[16]

IS DESIGN AN "UNSCIENTIFIC" EXPLANATION?

Some people automatically dismiss the idea of creation, saying that it's unscientific to consider such an alternative. The authors of *Teaching About Evolution*, for example, dismiss creation as "unscientific" and "religious." Why? Because, "basic proposals of creation science are not subject to test and verification."[17]

Consider this: just what is "science"? Clearly stated, "science" is the pursuit of knowledge about nature and the physical world. In this pursuit, any information from a reliable source (history, statistics, archeology, to name a few) must be considered. Ideally, scientific knowledge is something that can be monitored, repeated, and studied over and over again, just to be certain it is correct.

Science, however, has its limits. Normal science deals only with observable events in the present, not with unrepeatable events in the past. In the case of both creation and evolution, we're dealing with events that can neither be observed nor be repeated. Just like creation, evolution also, "is not subject to test and verification."

Two particular scientific principles apply to past events: Causality tells us that everything that has a beginning, including life and the universe, has a "cause." Analogy tells us that if intelligence is needed to generate information in the present, we can assume the same for the past. Building upon these principles, we can expect to find that life and the universe had a "cause," and that intelligent guidance was necessary.

Philosopher of science Stephen Meyer agrees that we must consider all the options:

We have not yet encountered any good in principle reason to exclude design from science. Design seems just as scientific (or unscientific) as its evolutionary competitors. . . .

An openness to empirical arguments for design is therefore a necessary condition of a fully rational historical biology. A rational, historical biology must not only address the question, "Which materialistic or naturalistic evolutionary scenario provides the most adequate explanation of biological complexity?" but also the question "Does a strictly materialistic evolutionary scenario or one involving intelligent agency or some other theory best explain the origin of biological complexity, given all relevant evidence?" To insist otherwise is to insist that materialism holds a metaphysically privileged position. Since there seems no reason to concede that assumption, I see no reason to concede that origins theories must be strictly naturalistic.[18]

The honest, objective scientist will agree. To be thorough in our evaluation of science and truth, we must consider all possible solutions and sources of information.

What Does "Creation" Look Like?

The arguments against evolution are impressive, and the possibility of creation is logical. But does looking at the world alone tell us whether or not it was "created"? To answer this question, we must first decide what we mean by the word. Every day we encounter objects and decide (usually subconsciously) whether they were created or not. We find a soda can, car keys, or sheet of paper on the ground and know immediately that they were designed and manufactured. A piece of rock or clod of dirt we know were not planned or built intentionally (by man).

A vast difference exists between an orchestra performing a score of music and the sound of a waterfall. A portrait painted by an artist is completely distinct from the results of a canvas left out on the ground. The texture of woven cloth is easily distinguishable from the feel of dirt in a garden.

We can tell the difference between created objects and those which are not by the amount of information they contain. Created objects possess what is termed specified complexity — information arranged in such a way that it could not possibly have appeared by chance. It is hopeless that a soda can or a score of music could emerge on their own. The amount of complex information they contain could only occur by design and intentional production.[19]

There is also an important difference between order and complexity. Nature has some examples of order in it, such as the repetitive sequence of crystals in ice or granite rock. But this kind of order does not contain the complexity of, say, a set of car keys or a computer chip.

The Search for Extraterrestrial Intelligence program (SETI) is a terrific example of our attempts to distinguish randomness from intelligence. Outer space produces a great amount of electronic "noise." The SETI program seeks to pick out signals that are neither random nor a repetitive sequence (such as that produced by pulsars). Rather, they are attempting to find signals containing a high level of specified complexity. Why? Because such signals could only be produced by an intelligent being.

CREATION IN LIFE

Living creatures house vast amounts of specified complexity. The DNA of their cells contains almost infinite quantities of specific information, directing the cells to work in concert and perform defined roles. The design of a creature's organs also shows intent and purpose of function, as well as complex interdependency upon one another.

All this is counter to one of the basic laws of physics: the second law of thermodynamics:

> Complex ordered arrangements and systems naturally become simpler and more disorderly (increased entropy or randomness) with time.

Left on their own, objects become more disorganized over time. It's a rule of nature. Evolution somehow tries to portray a universe that, on its own, becomes ever more orderly and more complex. Evolutionists see humans and other advanced creatures as examples of this increasing complexity. Yet the laws of physics state just the opposite. Consider just some of the elaborate behavior and features of living creatures:

- The inexplicable metamorphosis of a butterfly
- The map-like, highly technical, computerized dance of the honey bee
- The incredible transcontinental flight of the migratory duck and goose to the exact spot of their birth as a tiny duckling or gosling

- The unduplicable flight mechanics of a bird
- The highly technical communication skills of a dolphin
- The incredible genetics of a tadpole-frog amphibian

Intricate and wonderful structures are found in living creatures. Lobster eyes, for example, are modeled on a perfect square with precise geometrical relationships. The lobster's eye design was copied by NASA in the construction of x-ray telescopes.[20]

Research has discovered that the nervous system of leeches uses mathematical calculations to command the movement of its muscles.[21]

Bats are endowed with a finely sensitive sonar system, able to detect an object as fine as a human hair from among its surroundings. To accomplish this, their sonar distinguishes ultra-sound echoes only 2 to 3 millionths of a second apart. Compare this with the fact that man-made sonar can distinguish echoes only 12 millionths of a second apart.[22]

Realizing that evolution has limits on what it could possibly accomplish, the famous British evolutionist J.B.S. Haldane claimed in 1949 that evolution could never produce "various mechanisms, such as the wheel and magnet, which would be useless till fairly perfect."[23]

In his estimation, the presence of these structures in living creatures would prove evolution impossible, for evolution could never "create" such things. But today we know that some living creatures have "wheels" within them. The rotary motor that turns the flagellum of some bacterium is a fine example of a living wheel.[24]

Other creatures such as turtles,[25] Monarch butterflies,[26] and bacteria[27] rely upon magnetic sensors within their bodies for navigation from place to place. These wheels and magnets, in Haldane's own words, discredit the very theory he spent a lifetime teaching.

Apart from other arguments, living things qualify as being created simply on the basis of their specified complexity. No other explanation is really necessary.

No Surprise: Life with Similarities

Evolutionists look at the similarities between creatures, and abstractly insist that one must have transformed into another. But there is another reasonable explanation: They have a common Designer and Creator.

It just makes sense. Mazda automobiles all have four wheels, one engine, and the Mazda logo. Why? Because a Mazda 323 evolved into a Mazda 626 and then into a Mazda 929? The likelihood seems pretty remote. What's more, searching junkyards for "fossils" of Mazda transitional form has turned up no evidence to support this idea.

Rather, Mazdas are alike because they have a common designer and manufacturer. In the same way, we shouldn't be surprised if the designer of living creatures used similar biochemistry and physical structures in a variety of living beings.

Don Boys, in his book *Evolution: Fact, Fraud, or Faith?* points out the proper role of similarity:

> Similarity does not equal relationship. Evolutionists often use similarity between animals and man to "prove" Darwinism. They point to the legs, neck, ears, etc. of apes and remind us how similar they are to those of men. Creationists likewise use similarities to support creation. . . . So God used His blueprint for many of His creatures. Similarities don't mean common ancestry but a common architect![28]

CREATION IN OUR UNIVERSE

Does our universe (the layout of the planets and stars) show specified complexity? Does it show signs that could only result from the work of a creator? Consider some of the facts:

- The universe has at least 100 billion galaxies.
- The Milky Way Galaxy alone has 100 billion stars.
- Our own galaxy is so large, if the earth and sun were only one foot apart, you would have to travel 25,000 miles to reach the center of the galaxy.
- Our solar system hurls through space at 600,000 mph.
- The earth rotates on its axis at 1,000 mph.
- The earth moves around the sun at 70,000 mph.
- Earth is 93,000,000 miles from the sun. If it were seven million miles closer or seven million miles farther away, humans would instantly either burn to death or freeze to death.
- The moon is 240,000 miles from the earth. If it were only 50,000 miles closer to the earth, our ocean tides would cover almost all of the landmasses by 35–50 feet, twice a day.[29]

Learning about the planets in our solar system gives us just a glimpse of the true uniqueness of Earth. Outer space contains many hazards: extreme

The Milky Way Galaxy.

temperatures, deadly cosmic radiation, meteors and asteroids, lethal gases, enormous pressures, and tremendous gravity — all causing death to any living thing that becomes exposed.

Yet our planet Earth provides remarkable protection from all these hazards. Not only do we have protection, we also have water and food and material resources, everything needed to thrive. Nowhere in the universe have astronomers observed another environment that at all approaches the idealness of Earth. It's no wonder that life flourishes here, and nowhere else.

One of America's leading space scientists, Dr. Wernher von Braun, affirmed the design inherent in our universe:

> One cannot be exposed to the law and order of the universe without concluding that there must be design and purpose behind it all. . . . The better we understand the intricacies of the universe and all it harbors, the more reason we have found to marvel at the inherent design upon which it is based.[30]

One of the greatest scientists of all time, Isaac Newton, discovered many physical laws of the universe and also saw magnificence in its design:

This most beautiful system of the sun, planets, and comets could only proceed from the counsel and dominion of an intelligent and powerful Being.[31]

Isaac Newton, like most early scientists, understood that the earth was created.

OUR UNIVERSE WAS "READY-MADE"

There exist several constants, or characteristics, that make life feasible. A small change in one or another of them would make life totally impossible on earth, or anywhere else in the universe. It almost seems as though the laws of physics themselves are precisely "tuned" so as to favor the maintenance of life. This "life supporting" character of the universe is called the "anthropic principle." To put it another way, without the right kind of physics you don't get physicists.

Is it possible that our ideal earth came into existence through random chance? Or is there a Designer and Creator behind it all? The question is similar to the probability of life arising on its own. The calculated statistical chance of our ideal planet forming at random is greater than 10^{1000} power. And as Dr. Emile Borel explains, anything with a chance of less than 1 in 10^{50} would never happen no matter how much time there is.[32]

The only reasonable explanation for the existence of order in the universe and our unique planet is intentional creation. Many scientists, some of whom are atheists themselves, agree.

Bert Thompson, Ph.D. and Wayne Jackson, M.A.: "The entire universe was made for man."[33]

Dr. John Gribbin, world-renowned cosmologist: "Our universe seems to be tailor-made for us."[34]

Dr. Robert Jastrow, founder of NASA Space Studies: "The anthropic principle is the most theistic (God-supporting) result ever to come out of science."[35]

Dr. Freeman Dyson of Princeton University: "The universe must have known we were coming."[36]

Just as in living creatures, the universe also shows specified complexity — complexity that can only result from an intentional creator.

LEADERS OF SCIENCE WHO UPHOLD CREATION

Literally thousands and thousands of scientists worldwide, though muted from some textbooks, see intelligent design in our universe. They applied their unique field of science to the origin of life, and planets and stars, and are convinced there is a Creator behind it all.

Dean H. Kenyon, professor of biology at San Francisco State University, is a noted scientist who clearly believes that creationism is both scientific and reasonable:

> It is my conviction that if any professional biologist will take adequate time to examine carefully the assumptions upon which the macro-evolutionary doctrine rests, and the observational and laboratory evidence that bears on the problem of origins, he/she will conclude that there are substantial reasons for doubting the truth of this doctrine. Moreover, I believe that a scientifically sound creationist view of origins is not only possible, but is to be preferred over the evolutionary view.[37]

Other well-known scientists also uphold creation as the only logical, believable explanation. They include some of the following, listed along with their field of research:

Louis Agazzi — developed the study of glacial geology and ichthyology.

Charles Babbage — developed the science of computers and developed actuarial tables and the calculating machine.

Francis Bacon — developed the scientific method.

Robert Boyle — developed the sciences of chemistry and gas dynamics.

David Brewster — developed the science of optical mineralogy.

Georges Cuvier — developed the sciences of comparative anatomy and vertebrate paleontology.

Humphry Davy — developed the science of thermokinetics.

Albert Einstein — developed the law of relativity. Selected as

"Person of the Century" by *Time* magazine.

Henri Fabre — developed the science of insect entomology.

Michael Faraday — developed the science of electromagnetics; developed the field theory; invented the electric generator.

Ambrose Fleming — developed the science of electronics; invented thermionic valve which made possible high-quality radio broadcasting.

Joseph Henry — invented the electric motor and the galvanometer; discovered self-induction.

William Herschel — developed the science of galactic astronomy; discovered double stars; developed the Global Star Catalog.

James P. Joule — developed reversible thermodynamics.

Johann Kepler — developed the science of physical astronomy; developed the ephemeris tables.

Carolus Linnaeus — developed the sciences of taxonomy and systematic biology; developed the classification system.

Joseph Lister — developed the science of antiseptic surgery.

Matthew Maury — developed the science of oceanography; hydrography.

James Clerk Maxwell — developed the science of electrodynamics.

Gregor Mendel — founded the modern science of genetics.

Samuel F.B. Morse — invented the telegraph.

Isaac Newton — developed the science of dynamics and the discipline of calculus; father of the law of gravity; invented the reflecting telescope.

Blaise Pascal — developed the science of hydrostatics; invented the barometer.

Louis Pasteur — developed the science of bacteriology; discovered the law of biogenesis; invented fermentation control; developed vaccination and immunizations.

William Ramsay — discovered the inert gases.

John Ray — developed the science of biology and natural science.

Lord Raleigh — developed the science of dimensional analysis.

Bernhard Riemann — developed non-Euclidean geometry.

James Simpson — developed the field of gynecology; developed the use of chloroform.

Nicholas Steno — developed the science of stratigraphy.

George Stokes — developed the science of fluid mechanics.

William Thompson (Lord Kelvin) — developed the sciences of thermodynamics and energetics; invented the absolute temperature
scale; developed the trans-Atlantic cable.
Leonardo Da Vinci — developed the science of hydraulics.
Rudolph Virchow — developed the science of pathology.
John Woodward — developed the science of paleontology.
Sir Fred Hoyle — well-known British mathematician, astronomer,
and cosmologist; author of *Evolution from Space*; knighted by
the queen of England for scientific excellence and integrity.

To the objective, unbiased mind, creation is everywhere evident. Scientist Allan Sandage was overwhelmed by this truth:

> The world is too complicated in all its parts and interconnec-
> tions to be due to chance alone. I am convinced that the existence
> of life with all its order in each of its organisms is simply too well
> put together. Each part of a living thing depends on all its other
> parts to function. How does each part know? How is each part
> specified at conception? The more one learns of biochemistry the
> more unbelievable it becomes unless there is some type of orga-
> nizing principle — an architect.[38]

Summary

Only two alternatives exist to explain the origin of life. Either we evolved
from dead material or we were intentionally designed and created. There
are no other options. Objective science demonstrates that our universe, and
the life it contains, could not possibly have originated by chance. The theory
of evolution with its spontaneous generation, random mutation, natural
selection, enormous time, and fossil evidence is actually an ideal without
support.

Instead, the evidence points directly toward intentional design and
creation. Created objects contain what is termed specified complexity,
information arranged in such a way that it could not possibly have appeared by chance. The order and complexity of our universe and all living things is very great; so great that the probability of it happening by
chance is zero. The fact that living things have similarities with one another indicates they have a common designer, not that one evolved into
the other.

Neither is it "unscientific" to consider creation as a possibility. The most reliable scientific research can only be done on events in the present. Still, enormous evidence remains from past events. Such evidence has caused many of the greatest scientists in history to affirm creation as the only reasonable answer to the existence of life.

ENDNOTES

1 Robert Jastrow, "God's Creation," *Science Digest* (Special Spring Issue 1980): p. 68.
2 Wayne Jackson, *Evolution Revolution* (Montgomery, AL: Apologetics Press, Inc., 1994), quoting William Fix, *The Bone Peddlers* (New York, NY: Macmillan, 1984), p. 179–180.
3 Dr. Colin Patterson in an interview on British Broadcasting Corporation (BBC) television (March 4, 1982).
4 J.W.G. Johnson, *Evolution?* (Los Angeles, CA: Perpetual Eucharistic Adoration, 1986), p. 3.
5 Brian Leith, *The Descent of Darwin: A Handbook of Doubts about Darwinism* (London: Collins, 1982), p. 11.
6 Pierre-Paul Grassé, *Evolution of Living Organisms* (New York, NY: Academic Press, 1977), p. 8.
7 Dr. S. Lovtrup, *Darwinism: The Refutation of a Myth* (London: Croom Helmm, 1987), p. 422. *Los Angeles Examiner* (January 7, 1970).
8 Hsu, "Darwin's Three Mistakes," *Geology*, v. 14, p. 534 (1986).
9 Paul S. Taylor, *Origins Answer Book* (Mesa, AZ: Eden Productions, 1990), p. 49.
10 Richard Dawkins, *The Blind Watchmaker* (New York, NY: W.W. Norton, 1986), p. 130.
11 Ibid., p.130.
12 "Science and Faith," *New Man* (September/October 1999).
13 Sir Fred Hoyle and Chandra Wickramasinghe, *Evolution from Space* (London: J.M. Dent & Sons, Ltd., 1981), p. 141, 144.
14 Paul Davies, "The Christian Perspective of a Scientist," *New Scientist* (June 2, 1983): p. 638.
15 H.S. Lipson, "A Physicist Looks at Evolution," *Physics Bulletin*, vol. 31 (1980): p. 138.
16 Leonard Huxley, editor, *Life and Letters of Thomas Henry Huxley* (New York, NY: D. Appleton, 1909), p. 241.
17 National Academy of Science, *Teaching About Evolution and the Nature of Science* (Washington, DC: National Academy Press, 1998).
18 J.P. Moreland, editor, *The Creation Hypothesis*, "The Methodological Equivalence of Design and Descent: Can There Be a 'Scientific Theory of Creation'?" by S.C. Meyer (Downers Grove, IL: InterVarsity Press, 1994) p. 98, 102.
19 K. Ham, "How Would You Answer . . . ?" *Creation Ex Nihilo*, 20(3):32-34 (June–August 1998).
20 M. Chown, "X-ray Lens Brings Finer Chips into Focus," *New Scientist*, 151(2037):18 (July 6, 1996).
21 R. Howlett, "Simple Minds," *New Scientist*, 158(2139):28–32 (June 20, 1998). The editorial on p. 3 of the same issue displays its materialistic bias by asserting, without the slightest evidence: "The leech's nerve cells arrived at trigonometry by an obviously random and undirected search — evolution, whereas humans seem to have acquired math by intellectual effort."
22 P. Weston, "Bats: Sophistication in Miniature," *Creation Ex Nihilo*, 21(l):28–31 (December 1998–February 1999).
23 D. Dewar, L.M. Davies, and J.B.S. Haldane, *Is Evolution a Myth? A Debate Between D. Dewar and L.M. Davies vs. J.B.S. Haldane* (London: Watts & Co. Ltd / Paternoster Press, 1949), p. 90.
24 J.D. Sarfati, "Design in Living Organisms: Motors," *Creation Ex Nihilo Technical Journal*, 12(t):3–5 (1998).
25 "Turtles — Reading Magnetic Maps," *Creation Ex Nihilo* 21(2):30 (March–May 1999).

26 A.H. Poirier, "The Magnificent Migrating Monarch," *Creation Ex Nihilo*, 20(l):28–31 (December 1997–February 1998). But monarchs only use the earth's magnetic field to give them the general direction, while they rely on the sun's position for most of their navigation.

27 M. Helder, "The World's Smallest Compasses," *Creation Ex Nihilo*, 20(2):5253 (March–May 1998).

28 Don Boys, *Evolution: Fact, Fraud, or Faith?* (Largo, FL: Freedom Publications, 1994), p. 112.

29 Cressy Morrison, *Readers Digest* (December, 1946).

30 Remarks taken from *Applied Christianity* (May 1974): p. 8.

31 N. Geisler and J.K. Anderson, *Origin Science* (1987): p. 122.

32 Emile Borel, *Probabilities and Life* (New York, NY: Dover Publications, 1962).

33 Bert Thompson and Wayne Jackson, *The Case for the Existence of God* (Montgomery, AL: Apologetics Press, Inc., 1996), p. 19–20.

34 John Gribbin, *Genesis: The Origins of Man and the Universe* (New York, NY: Delacorte Press, 1981), p. 309.

35 Robert Jastrow, *The Astronomer and God, Intellectuals Speak Out About God* (New York, NY: Regenery Gateway, 1984), p. 21–22.

36 Freeman Dyson, *Scientific American* (September 1971): p. 50.

37 D.H. Kenyon, "The Creationist View of Biological Origins," *NEX4 Journal* (Spring 1984): p. 33.

38 Allan Sandage, "A Scientist Reflects on Religious Belief," *Truth*, vol. 1 (1985): p. 54.

CHAPTER 7

WHY IS EVOLUTION SO ATTRACTIVE?

EVOLUTION: A FAIRY TALE FOR GROWN-UPS

Evolution, in almost every school, is taught as a fact of life. Yet we know that the scientific support for evolution is quite shaky. Since this is the case, we must ask, "What is it about evolution that's so attractive? Why do so many people cling to a theory that is based upon so little evidence? Why is it taught so persistently in spite of the facts?"

Just to be fair, it's good to remember that Charles Darwin was writing in the mid-1800s, about the time of the Civil War. His concept seemed reasonable to some people; lifeless matter and energy gave rise to simple life, and that simple life gradually evolved into higher life forms. Amoeba grew into jelly-fish, to vertebrate fish, to amphibians, to reptiles, to birds, to mammals, and on to man.

Darwin wrote without the benefit of modern science, without a laboratory to test his ideas, initially without even professional colleagues with whom to critique his theory. Scientific knowledge and communication has expanded exponentially since the time of Darwin, proving his claims entirely unfounded.

Consider some of the conclusions of our most noted scientists. Professor Louis Bounoure, former president of the Biological Society of Strasbourg and director of the Strasbourg Zoological Museum, contends that:

> Evolution is a fairy tale for grown-ups. This theory has helped nothing in the progress of science. It is useless.[1]

Dr. T.N. Tahmisian of the United States Atomic Energy Commission declares:

> Scientists who go about teaching that evolution is a fact of life are great con-men, and the story they are telling may be the greatest hoax ever. In explaining evolution, we do not have one iota of fact.[2]

Paul Lemoine, director of the Natural History Museum in Paris and the editor of the *Encyclopedie Francaise*, recognized the lack of evidence for evolution as early as 1937:

> The theories of evolution, with which our studious youth have been deceived, constitute actually a dogma that all the world continues to teach: but each, in his specialty, the zoologist or the botanist, ascertains that none of the explanations furnished is adequate. . . . It results from this summary, that the theory of evolution is impossible.[3]

H.S. Lipson, a British physicist and Fellow of the Royal Society, wrote:

> I have always been slightly suspicious of the theory of evolution because of its ability to account for any property of living beings (the long neck of the giraffe, for example). I have therefore tried to see whether biological discoveries over the last thirty years or so fit in with Darwin's theory. I do not think that they do. . . . To my mind, the theory does not stand up at all.[4]

Malcolm Muggeridge, world famous journalist and philosopher, anticipates the future reputation of evolution:

> I myself am convinced that the theory of evolution, especially the extent to which it's been applied, will be one of the great jokes in the history books of the future.[5]

Over time, Darwin himself developed increasing doubts about the truth of his own theory. Loren Eisley provides a critique of Darwin's writings:

> A close examination of the last edition of the *Origin* reveals that in attempting on scattered pages to meet the objections being launched against his theory, the much labored-upon volume had

become contradictory. . . . The last repairs to the *Origin* reveal . . . how very shaky Darwin's theoretical structure had become. His gracious ability to compromise had produced some striking inconsistencies. His book was already a classic, however, and these deviations for the most part passed unnoticed even by his enemies.[6]

However, in spite of the growing scientific evidence to the contrary, the popularity of evolution continues to grow and grow.

No Longer a Theory: The "Hypothesis of Evolution"

In scientific research we have essentially three levels of confidence: hypothesis, theory, and law:

- **Hypothesis.** A hypothesis is simply a proposal, a possibility that requires an answer. To say, for example, that milk is made from limestone because they are both white in color, is a hypothesis. Whether or not it is true can then be tested. In the case of milk and limestone, we already know the answer, and the hypothesis is false.

- **Theory.** A theory is an idea that has already been tested, and so far has been found to be correct, but not all the information is in yet. Significant questions still remain, and further testing is needed.

- **Law.** A law is an idea that has been thoroughly tested with every known method, and has been found absolutely true — entirely flawless. The law of gravity, for example, is 100 percent true, every time, every place (on earth), and with every person.

If the evidence continues to support an idea, it will progress from being just a hypothesis, to being recognized as a theory, and then universally accepted as a law. The concept of relativity (the relationships between time, speed, matter, and energy) began as a hypothesis. As Einstein researched his hypothesis, he found it correctly explained the things he observed in the universe.

As support for the hypothesis of relativity grew, it was upgraded to a theory, the theory of relativity, first published in 1915. Since that time, the theory of relativity has been applied and tested in thousands of ways, thousands of times. And, like gravity, has proven itself 100 percent true, every time, every place, and with every person. So today, instead of referring to it as a theory, we speak of the law of relativity.

Darwin's idea has been known for 140 years as the theory of evolution, meaning that it has supposedly been found correct so far. And yet, evolution is not taught as a theory, but as a law.

This is a crime against scientific reason. These 140 years of research have not uncovered anything in the way of support for evolution. We can no longer justifiably call it a theory. Evolution is no more than a hypothesis — a hypothesis that so far has been found without support.

The co-holder of the 1945 Nobel Prize for developing penicillin, Sir Ernst Chain, determined natural selection by chance mutations a "hypothesis based on no evidence and irreconcilable with the facts." He continued, "These classical evolutionary theories are a gross over-simplification of an immensely complex and intricate mass of facts, and it amazes me that they are swallowed so uncritically and readily, and for such a long time, by so many scientists without a murmur of protest."[7]

G.A. Kerkut, himself an evolutionist, recognized this fact long ago, but his claims were largely ignored:

> There is the theory that all the living forms in the world have arisen from a single source which itself came from an inorganic form. This theory can be called the "general theory of evolution," and the evidence which supports this is not sufficiently strong to allow us to consider it as anything more than a working hypothesis.[8]

Why isn't the scientific community more straightforward with the lack of evidence for evolution? It's time we insist the truth be told!

EVOLUTION: IT'S A PHILOSOPHY

In spite of the facts, the voice of Darwin's "dead" theory is heard throughout the world, thousands of times every day. Arthur Koestler, British novelist, clearly sums up the status of evolution in our culture:

> In the meantime, the educated public continues to believe that Darwin has provided all the relevant answers by the magic formula of random mutation plus natural selection, quite unaware of the fact that random mutations turned out to be irrelevant and natural selection a tautology.[9]

Why? Why is an idea with so little merit clung to so strongly? Why do some people persist in clinging to evolution as fact when so little proof exists? The answer is this: Evolution is the only way to explain life without giving credit to God.

If evolution's leaders admit that life was created, they also must admit there exists a Creator. And if people admit there is a Creator, they might have to change their lives. They might have to be accountable to a greater power. Change is often uncomfortable and obedience means giving up on personal pride and arrogance.

It comes as no surprise that most evolutionists are also atheists or agnostics. A recent survey, for example, was published in the journal *Nature* documenting the religious makeup of the National Academy of Sciences, an organization exclusively committed to propagating evolution. One half of all 517 NAS members in biological and physical sciences responded: 72.2 % were overtly atheistic, 20.8 % agnostic, and only 7.0 % believed in a personal God. In fact, belief in God was lowest among biologists.[10]

Evolution is so popular not because it meets the rigorous standards of science, but because it fits the world view, the philosophy, of these people. They find the concept of God bewildering, challenging, or even aggravating. So, it seems natural to try and find ways to explain their existence without God. Evolution appears as a ready-made answer to one of the biggest questions: existence. Evolution is a way to explain everything without God. It helps atheists defend their own existence, and still be consistent with their "religion" of a godless universe.[11]

Many observers agree. The famous Nobel Prize-winning scientist from Harvard, Dr. George Wald, enlightens the honest student with the underlying bias which causes the rapid proliferation of Darwin's theory in the hallways of science:

> When it comes to the origin of life on this earth, there are only two possibilities: creation or spontaneous generation (evolution). There is no third way. Spontaneous generation was disproved 100 years ago, but that leads us only to one other conclusion: that of supernatural creation. We cannot accept that on philosophical

grounds (personal reasons), therefore, we choose to believe the impossible: that life arose spontaneously by chance.[12]

Dr. Wald goes on to explain the total absurdity of "faith" in evolution:

> Most modern biologists, having reviewed with satisfaction the downfall of the spontaneous generation hypothesis, yet unwilling to accept the alternative belief in special creation, are left with nothing.[13]

H.S. Lipson, professor of physics, University of Manchester, sees the metaphysical basis of evolution:

> In fact, evolution became in a sense a scientific religion; almost all scientists have accepted it and many are prepared to "bend" their observations to fit in with it.[14]

Harold Urey, Nobel Prize laureate, recognized power of his "faith" in evolution in spite of its impossibility:

> All of us who study the origin of life find that the more we look into it, the more we feel it is too complex to have evolved anywhere. We all believe as an article of faith that life evolved from dead matter on this planet. It is just that life's complexity is so great, it is hard for us to imagine that it did.[15]

Pierre-Paul Grassé, of the University of Paris and past-president of the French Academy of Sciences, comments on people's dedication to sectarianism (life without God) in spite of the lack of evidence for evolution:

> The deceit is sometimes unconscious, but not always, since some people, owing to their sectarianism, purposely overlook reality and refuse to acknowledge the inadequacies and the falsity of their beliefs.[16]

E.J.H. Corner, professor of tropical botany at Cambridge University, confesses:

> I still think that, to the unprejudiced, the fossil record of plants is in favor of special creation . . . yet mutations and natural selection are the bricks with which the taxonomist has built his temple of evolution, and where else have we to worship?[17]

Well-known scientist Heribert Nilsson of Lund University spent his entire career trying to artificially foster evolution between creatures. He concluded that the idea was more like a religion than a science:

> My attempts to demonstrate evolution by an experiment carried on for more than 40 years have completely failed. . . . It is not even possible to make a caricature of an evolution out of paleobiological facts. . . . The idea of an evolution rests on pure belief![18]

Professor Richard Lewontin, a geneticist, is a renowned leader in promoting the concept of evolutionary biology. He recently penned this very revealing statement that demonstrates his prejudice against creation, regardless of whether or not the facts support it. The italics were in the original publication:

> We take the side of science *in spite* of the patent absurdity of some of its constructs, *in spite* of its failure to fulfill many of its extravagant promises of health and life, *in spite* of the tolerance of the scientific community for unsubstantiated just-so stories, because we have a prior commitment, a *commitment to materialism*. It is not that the methods and institutions of science somehow compel us to accept a material explanation of the phenomenal world, but, on the contrary, that we are forced by our a priori adherence to material causes to create an apparatus of investigation and a set of concepts that produce material explanations, no matter how counter-intuitive, no matter how mystifying to the uninitiated. Moreover, that materialism is an absolute, for we cannot allow a Divine Foot in the door.[19]

Darwin was initially trained to be a minister. Paradoxically, however, he developed a disdain for faith in Jesus Christ. That capsule of inner rebellion seemed to grow over the years until it permeated his entire being with a sense of anger; even hatred. Darwin seemed obsessed with living apart from any reference to God. *Encyclopedia Britannica* opens a candid window into Darwin's restless soul when it quotes him as saying:

> The Old Testament, from its manifestly false history of the earth, was no more to be trusted than the sacred books of the Hindus, or the beliefs of any barbarian. The New Testament is a

damnable doctrine. (I can) hardly see how anyone ought to wish Christianity to be true.[20]

Every person has a world view; a basic set of assumptions used to interpret what's happening around them. The assumption used by evolutionists is naturalism. This is the world view that assumes up front there is no God and no act of creation. Instead, everything has come about by chance alone.

Closely related to naturalism is the philosophy called humanism. The first two tenets of the Humanist Manifesto II, signed in 1973 by many well-known evolutionists, are these:

- Humanists regard the universe as self-existing and not created.
- Humanism believes that Man is a part of nature and has emerged as a result of a continuous process.

Clearly, without a commitment to evolution (even if it defies the evidence) the basic principles of naturalism and humanism would be negated. This commitment was plainly stated by one of the leading biologists and science writers of his day, Professor D.M.S. Watson:

> Evolution [is] a theory universally accepted not because it can be proven by logically coherent evidence to be true, but because the only alternative, special creation, is clearly incredible.[21]

Why aren't more scientists more open to considering the evidence against evolution? Dean Kenyon, a professor of biology at San Francisco State University, admits that many scientists refuse to study problems with evolution because it "would open the door to the possibility (or the necessity) of supernatural origins of life."[22]

Science demands that scientists remain consistent in their reasoning. When an object shows specified complexity, it indicates that a Designer and Creator must exist. When, for example, a piece of molded pottery is discovered, it's obvious the object must have been designed, even though the designer it not present. Yet we have today a naturalistic bias among many scientists, causing them to reject an intelligent source as the designer of the literally encyclopedic information carried in every living cell.

Julian Huxley is one of the best-known naturalists and humanist philosophers. Notice his presentation of the religion of evolution:

Adapted from an illustration in a current high school biology textbook.

In the evolutionary pattern of thought there is no longer either need or room for the supernatural. The earth was not created, it evolved. So did all the animals and plants that inhabit it, including our human selves, mind and soul as well as brain and body. So did religion.[23]

The real reason for rejecting the creation explanation is the commitment to naturalism, commitment to finding life without God. Commitment to naturalism causes people to deny the evidence and hold to unsupportable claims, such as dead matter giving rise to life, single-celled organisms transforming into apes, and ape-like creatures developing into humans.

ZEALOTS, HALLUCINATIONS, AND PROPAGANDA

Remember what a hallucination is? Seeing, hearing, and believing things that do not actually exist. Yet those holding on to evolution are not only themselves hallucinating, but enthusiastically encouraging — even demanding — that others do the same.

Many humanist leaders are very intent and outspoken about using our schools to radically promote their philosophy:

I am convinced that the battle for humankind's future must be waged and won in the public school classroom by teachers who correctly perceive their role as the proselytizers of a new faith: a religion of humanity that recognizes and respects the spark of what theologians call divinity in every human being. These teachers must embody the same selfless dedication as the most rabid fundamentalist preachers, for they will be ministers of another sort, utilizing a classroom instead of a pulpit to convey humanist values in whatever subject they teach, regardless of the educational level, preschool day care or large state university. The classroom must and will become an arena of conflict between the old and the new, the rotting corpse of Christianity, together with all its adjacent evils and misery, and the new faith of humanism. . . .

It will undoubtedly be a long, arduous, painful struggle replete with much sorrow and many tears, but humanism will emerge triumphant. It must if the family of humankind is to survive.[24]

Notice the fervor in the author's voice. *Teaching about Evolution*, published by the National Academy of Sciences, goes so far as to demand that all references to creation be removed:

Statements about creation . . . should not be regarded as reasonable alternatives to scientific explanations for the origin and evolution of life.[25]

Some humanist/evolutionist leaders, however, realize that if their blatant atheism were known, it would repel many American parents. Agnostic philosopher Ruse realized this risk and admonished:

"Evolution as a scientific theory makes a commitment to a kind of naturalism" but this "may not be a good thing to admit in a court of law."[26]

Nevertheless, the staunch support for teaching of evolution will likely continue as long as the public shows no objection. Dr. Alfred Rehwinkel summed it up very well:

Meanwhile, their [evolutionists'] unproven theories will continue to be accepted by the learned and the illiterate alike as absolute truth, and will be defended with a fanatic intolerance that has a parallel only in the bigotry of the darkest Middle Ages. If one does not accept evolution as an infallible dogma, implicitly and without question, one is regarded as an unenlightened ignoramus or is merely ignored as an obscurantist or a naive, uncritical fundamentalist.[27]

When objecting to teaching about creation, humanists and evolutionists often say that it would be in fact teaching "religion," since creation implies a supernatural Creator. And "religion," they contend, cannot be taught in school. Therefore, their reasoning goes, creation cannot be mentioned. Two points need to be understood:

- The difference between a "philosophy" like humanism and naturalism, and a "religion" is not definable. Both describe a particular way of viewing the world, history, human nature, and morality. A "religion" may or may not include reference to a supernatural being. Beyond this trait, however, "philosophy" and a "religion" are largely indistinguishable. Buddhism, as an example, is recognized as a "religion." But it has no "god" and its teachings are recognized as "philosophy."
- The scientific support for creation and arguments against evolution can stand alone. They do not rely upon any particular philosophy, religion, or even world view for adequate defense.

We who study in schools, teach in schools, lead the schools, and select the textbooks must be well aware of the evolutionist's true intent: indoctrination with the philosophies of naturalism and humanism.

EVOLUTION'S NUCLEAR FALLOUT

The impact of evolution on our society should never be underestimated; a point emphasized by Rene Dubos, one of America's top ecologists:

Most enlightened persons now accept as a fact that everything in the cosmos from heavenly bodies to human beings has developed and continues to develop through evolutionary processes. The great religions of the West have come to accept a historical view of creation. Evolutionary concepts are applied also to social institutions and to the arts. Indeed, most political parties, as well as schools of theology, sociology, history, or arts, teach these concepts and make them the basis of their doctrines.[28]

However unrelated, the concept of progressive development through errors or "mutations," and workability or "natural selection" has been applied to everything from religion to rap music. Many people believe that humans evolved from apes and lower animals. So what? Does it really matter today where we really came from? Does the truth about evolution and creation have any real impact on our daily lives?

Yes, absolutely.

From a strictly scientific point of view, emphasis upon evolution has led to many false assumptions about biology, astronomy, anthropology, and paleontology. It has caused researchers to continue looking for evolution's answers in places where few will ever be found. But on a personal and social level, evolution has a particularly devastating implication, as destructive as nuclear fallout.

Fallout: Disrespect for Human Life

Say for a moment that people are indeed simply the result of slime and accidents of nature. While more intelligent than other animals, humans are still just animals. They have no more inherent value than horses, hamsters, or hedgehogs. If humans came from beasts, then dignity, fairness, kindness, honesty, faithfulness, and justice have no relevance.

An author for *Scientific American* provided this inspiring comment:

> Yes, we are all animals, descendants of a vast lineage of replicators sprung from primordial pond scum.[29]

The implications of this kind of thinking are illustrated by this conversation between Jaron Lanier, a computer scientist, and Richard Dawkins, an evolutionist and professor at Oxford:

> Lanier: "There's a large group of people who simply are uncomfortable with accepting evolution because it leads to what they

perceive as a moral vacuum, in which their best impulses have no basis in nature."

Dawkins: "All I can say is, that's just tough. We have to face up to the truth."[30]

If humans are nothing more than a chance rearrangement of matter, one can argue that humans may be treated just like animals. History is full of examples of individuals and governments who embraced evolution, viewed their people as only "accidents of nature," and accordingly treated them even worse than animals.

Devaluation of human life is a root cause of most of today's social problems, including child abuse, abortion, racism, sexual prejudice, domestic violence, theft, and certainly murder. If people are only animals, why should we expect anything better?

Adolf Hitler is a dramatic example of

Adolf Hitler

evolutionary thought in action. He stressed the idea of biological evolution as the most forceful weapon against traditional religion, and he repeatedly condemned Christianity for its opposition to the teachings of evolution. Hitler saw the German people in a struggle for domination and "survival of

Bodies at a Dachau gas chamber during the Holocaust.

the fittest." He justified decisions to exterminate millions of citizens in order to prove that his own people were indeed the strongest. Hitler even wrote a book about these convictions, titled *Mein Kampf*, which literally means, "My Struggle."

Author R.E.D. Clark correctly observes that:

> Adolf Hitler's mind was captivated by evolutionary thinking — probably since the time he was a boy. Evolutionary ideas — quite undisguised — lie at the basis of all that is worst in *Mein Kampf*. A few quotations, taken at random, will show how Hitler reasoned. . . . "He who would live must fight, he who does not wish to fight in the world where permanent struggle is the law of life, has not the right to exist."[31]

Certainly not all the evils of Hitler's reign can be blamed on his evolutionary ideas. But it is undeniable that human devaluation is a devastating outcome of evolutionary thinking, and Hitler swore by evolution, as did Mussolini, Marx, Engels, Stalin, and Mao.

DARWIN'S DOWNFALL

Given his low view of human value, it's no surprise that Darwin was also a racist. His deep prejudice against blacks is demonstrated in this quotation from his book *The Descent of Man:*

> At some future period, not very distant as measured by centuries, the civilized races of man will almost certainly exterminate, and replace, the savage races throughout the world. At the same time, the anthropomorphous apes . . . will no doubt be exterminated. The break between man and his nearest allies will then be wider, for it will intervene between man in a more civilized state, as we may hope, even than the Caucasian, and some ape as low as a baboon, instead of as now between the Negro or Australian and the gorilla.[32]

An example of this attitude in action is found in Darwin's interaction with some South American Indians during his trip on the ship *Beagle*. He described them as "the miserable inhabitants of Tierra del Fuego," that they were on a very low rung of the evolutionary ladder, and were nothing more than cannibals, almost beasts.

However, Roman Catholic scholar Paul Kildare wrote:

Charles Darwin

Darwin hardly saw an Indian at all, and could not speak one word of their language.[33]

Two Roman Catholic scientists, both on the staff of American and European universities, also visited the same Indians and stated:

> The Fuegian Indians were not cannibals; they believed in one Supreme Being, to whom they prayed with confidence; they had "high principles of morality."[34]

Darwin not only carried racist, white supremacy views, but also was deeply prejudiced against women. In *The Descent of Man* he also wrote:

> The chief distinction in the intellectual powers of the two sexes is shown by man's attaining to a higher eminence, in whatever he takes up, than can woman; whether requiring deep thought, reason, or imagination, or merely the use of the senses and hands. . . . The average of mental power in man must be above that of woman.[35]

And he continued:

> Thus man has ultimately become superior to woman, poetry, strength, voice, etc.[36]

Has teaching about evolution led people to become more understanding and empathetic toward one another? Certainly not. Evolution actually creates a false justification for people to follow their most destructive instincts and treat each other with contempt, as each person "struggles to survive." Evolution may be a "fairy tale for grown-ups," but it carries a moral implication even more destructive than a nuclear bomb.

CREATION'S SOCIAL OUTCOME

By contrast, the outcome of teaching about creation is much different. Instructing people, consistent with the truth, that they were carefully designed and intentionally created is a cornerstone of self-respect. Viewing yourself as a finely tuned machine, a carefully crafted work of art, an intricately programmed computer, and vastly expressive creature — all wrapped into one — is completely different than the view pushed by evolution.

Viewing one another in the same respectful and admiring way is another outcome of the truth about creation. Rather than seeing others as competitors in the struggle for survival, as accidental mutations, we can truthfully view other humans as the intricate, valuable, awesome beings they have been ever since creation.

An essential component to solving most social and behavioral problems lies in healthy self-respect and respect toward others. Teaching about evolution clearly undermines the value of self-respect, while emphasis on creation magnifies self-respect.

MORE FALLOUT: ELIMINATION OF GOD

The concept of God, of a Supreme Being, is at the heart of morality. If God has declared that certain things are true and false, right and wrong, then we have the foundation for ethics, for justice, and law. We have the great advantage of timeless principles that can be applied to all peoples, cultures, and nations.

But if there is no God, no absolute authority, then morality has no foundation. If there is no God, there are no universal criteria for true and false, right and wrong. Whatever ethics, justice, and law we develop are only relative to the values of those people at that time.

Evolution is centered on atheism; that is, life without God. It denies that God exists or has any part at all in our world. It teaches that we are utterly alone, struggling in the world where every man and woman must compete. Hardly neutral in its implications, the concept of evolution has likely driven more people away from trusting God than any other.

Sir Julian Huxley in his keynote address at the 1959 Darwinian Centennial declared:

> Darwin pointed out that no supernatural designer was needed; since natural selection could account for any known form

of life, there was no room for a supernatural agency in its evolution . . . we can dismiss entirely all idea of a supernatural overriding mind being responsible for the evolutionary process.[37]

And yet, as we'll discuss in the next chapter, God is a reality. God is not only the Creator but also the source of enormous strength, inspiration, compassion, and encouragement. And yet these are just the essential qualities that evolution and its proponents want to deny us. Embracing naturalism, in spite of its hopelessness, they want nothing more than for you and me to share in their loneliness and sorrow. And sadly, many people are choosing to do just this.

WHAT SHOULD WE DO?

An Associated Press/NBC national poll found that 86 percent of all Americans wanted the creation model taught alongside the evolution model in the public school. Only 8 percent wanted only evolution taught. Six percent could not decide. If there's so much support for teaching about creation, why do the textbooks persist in teaching only "that which is scientifically impossible"? Ultimately, it's because we the students, parents, and public leaders are letting them get by with it.

It's high time that we demand honesty in science and in teaching. Evolution should be downgraded to the hypothesis that it actually is. Evidence for and against evolution should be presented in our schools in a way that's consistent with the truth.

Creation must also be presented, along with its arguments and evidence. No apology should be made for the fact that creation implies a Creator. It is simply the truth, and no amount of "political correctness" should ever obscure the truth.

Failure to take a stand will continue to have tragic consequences on the impressionable minds of students. If they continue to be taught that they are no more than "replicators from the slime," will we be surprised if they become entangled in depression, drug abuse, and suicide? If we continue to allow the emptiness of evolution to be taught, shall we be stunned to find a generation marked by abortion, sexually transmitted diseases, and teenage pregnancy? If they are instructed that there is no God, no moral absolutes, no truly good or bad choices, should we be shocked if they choose a life of apathy, dishonesty, or selfishness?

The future need not be this way. We must demand that the truth be told in every home, in every school, in every university.

SUMMING UP

Evolution is an idea without adequate evidence, and does not qualify to be called a "theory." Rather, it should be degraded to only a "hypothesis."

Why, then, is this fragile idea so popular? The answer is this: evolution is the only way to explain life without giving credit to God. It is their commitment to the philosophy of naturalism, and bias against belief in God, that causes evolutionists to overlook the evidence for creation, ignore evolution's fallacies, and hold on to evolution anyway. Their objective is to promote this philosophy, and they have been largely successful.

But evolution and naturalism carry dangers. They create the basis for human disrespect, an attitude with often lethal consequences. The life of Darwin himself showed these characteristics. They also alienate people from any knowledge of or relationship with God.

What should be done? First, we must demand honesty: that the actual evidence for and against evolution must be taught in our schools. Creation should also be presented, along with its arguments and evidence. No apology is necessary for the fact that creation implies a Creator. It is simply the truth. Failure to take a stand will perpetuate the tragic outcomes of evolutionary teaching.

ENDNOTES

1 Louis Bounoure, *The Advocate* (March 8, 1984): p. 17.
2 N.J. Mitchell, *Evolution and the Emperor's New Clothes* (United Kingdom: Roydon Publications, 1982), title page, quoting T.N. Tahmisian, The *Fresno Bee*, August 10,1959.
3 Paul Lemoine, "Introduction: De L'Evolution?" *5 Encyclopedie Francaise* (1937), p. 6
4 H.S. Lipson, "A Physicist Looks at Evolution," *Physics Bulletin,* vol. 31 (1980): p. 138.
5 Malcolm Muggeridge, Pascall Lectures, University of Waterloo, Ontario, Canada.
6 Loren Eisley, *Darwin's Century* (Garden City, NY: Doubleday, 1959), p. 242.
7 D.T. Rosevear, "Scientists Critical of Evolution," *Evolution Protest Movement* pamphlet, no. 224 (July 1980), p. 4.
8 G.A. Kerkut, *Implications of Evolution* (Oxford, UK: Pergamon, 1960), p. 157.
9 Arthur Koestler, *Janus: A Summing Up* (New York, NY: Random House, 1978), p. 184–185.
10 E.J. Larson and L. Witham, "Leading Scientists Still Reject God," *Nature*, 394(6691):313 (July 23, 1998).
11 Richard Dawkins, *The Blind Watchmaker: Why the Evidence of Evolution Reveals a Universe without Design* (New York, NY: W.W. Norton, 1986), p. 6.
12 Scott Huse, *The Collapse of Evolution* (Grand Rapids, MI: Baker Book House, 1988), p. 3.
13 George Wald, "The Origin of Life," *Scientific American*, vol. 191(2) (August 1954): p. 46.
14 Lipson, "A Physicist Looks at Evolution," p. 138.
15 *Christian Science Monitor* (Jan. 4, 1962).

16 Pierre-Paul Grassé, *Evolution of Living Organisms* (New York, NY: Academic Press, 1977), p. 8.

17 Anna M. Macleod, editor, *Contemporary Botanical Thought,* "Evolution," by E.J.H. Corner (Edinburgh: Oliver and Boyd, for the Botanical Society of Edinburgh, 1961), p. 97.

18 H. Nilsson, *Synthetische Artbildung* (Lund, Sweden: C.W.K. Gleerup, 1953), p. 1185, 1212.

19 Richard Lewontin, "Billions and Billions of Demons," *The New York Review* (January 9, 1997), p. 31.

20 Charles Darwin, *The Origin of Species* (London: A.L. Burt, 1859).

21 D.M.S. Watson, "Adaptation," *Nature* (1929): 124:233.

22 Charles Thaxton, Walter Bradley, and Roger Olsen, *The Mystery of Life's Origin: Reassessing Current Theories* (New York, NY: Philosophical Library, 1984), foreword by Dean Kenyon.

23 Sol Tax, editor, *Issues in Evolution*, Vol. 3 of *Evolution After Darwin* (Chicago, IL: University of Chicago Press, 1960), p. 260, quoting Julian Huxley.

24 Wendell R. Bird, *Origin of the Species — Revisited,* Volume 2 (New York, NY: Philosophical Library, c. 1989), p. 257, quoting J. Dunphy, "A Religion for a New Age," *The Humanist* (Jan.-Feb. 1983): 23, 26.

25 National Academy of Science, *Teaching About Evolution and the Nature of Science* (Washington, DC: National Academy Press, 1998), p 129.

26 C. Wieland, "The Religious Nature of Evolution," *Creation Ex Nihilo Technical Journal*, 8(1):34, from a symposium titled "The New Anti-Evolutionism" (during the 1993 annual meeting of the American Association for the Advancement of Science).

27 Alfred Rehwinkel, *The Wonders of Creation* (Minneapolis, MN: Bethany Fellowship, 1974), p. 31.

28 Rene Dubos, "Humanistic Biology," *American Scientist* (March 1965): p. 6.

29 J. Horgan, "The New Social Darwinists," *Scientific American*, 273(4):150–157 (October 1995): p. 151.

30 "Evolution: The Dissent of Darwin," *Psychology Today* (January/February 1997): p. 62.

31 Robert E.D. Clark, *Darwin: Before and After* (London: Paternoster Press, 1948), p. 115.

32 Charles Darwin, *The Descent of Man* (New York, NY: D. Appleton, 1897), p. 241–242.

33 Paul Kildare, "Monkey Business," *Christian Order* (December 1982): p. 591.

34 Ibid.

35 Darwin, *The Descent of Man*, p. 586.

36 Ibid., p. 588.

37 Julian Huxley, *Issues Evolution*, edited by Sol Tax (Chicago, IL: University of Chicago Press, 1960), p. 45. Sir Julian Huxley, in his keynote address at the 1959 Darwinian Centennial.

CHAPTER 8

WHO IS THE CREATOR?

WILL THE REAL CREATOR PLEASE STEP UP?

Evolution has been publicized as the sole, scientific explanation for life. Yet, as we have seen, the theory is without defense, and its continued teaching is a root cause of numerous social and theological problems.

Instead, the scientific evidence points toward intentional design and creation. The enormous complexities of living creatures cannot be explained in any other way. But just who is the Creator?

At this point we are dealing with the supernatural, with knowledge and power beyond that of humans. Many different religious teachers and philosophers claim to have supernatural inspiration and insight into just how the world was created and how life was formed.

How can we possibly know whom to believe? Where do we go to look for the Creator? Let's begin by drawing some comparisons to our daily lives. We are constantly surrounded by people who try to convince us that what they say is true. Professors expound to captive audiences their "conclusions" about what really happened in history. The press competes for our attention as they try to sell the "facts" concerning a particular murder case or civil unrest. Religious leaders of all varieties urge us to consider their way as the "true way" to wholeness. Government officials, especially at election time, promote the "rightness" of their policies and programs.

How can we best judge the validity of what people are saying, or what we are considering for ourselves? What criteria do we use, consciously or not, to decide who is really worth listening to? Let us suggest several ways we might be convinced that a speaker is in fact credible and telling us the truth:

- **Character.** Does the speaker keep his or her promises? What is the quality of their personal relationships? We are much more likely to trust them if their private life is in order.

- **Qualifications.** Does the speaker have the experience, education, or other training that marks him or her as an expert on the subject? How do these credentials compare to those of other authorities?

- **Motive.** What does the speaker have to gain or lose for taking his or her position? We usually are more trusting when we don't perceive a motive for self-gain — no money, material, or even fame to be won for taking a stand. In fact, we may find them even more reputable if they risk losing something for the sake of their position.

- **Results.** What's the track record? Has the speaker's position been tested by many people, in diverse and difficult situations, over long periods of time? Does it still work well? If so, it may be more likely to hold true in the future.

- **Extraordinary evidence.** Is there any unique sign or event that might support the special quality of the messenger or the message? If so, heads up!

Actually, we use this kind of reasoning everyday as we listen to people and analyze their messages. None of us want to be misled or deceived! We want to pick out the phonies ahead of time.

Think of what you look for when choosing a doctor. Ideally, he or she has warm interpersonal skills (character). Their training and experience are excellent (qualifications). The fees charged to you are reasonable, and give no hint of taking advantage of your illness for financial gain (motive). And, the physician you choose has a good reputation among people who have been helped in the past (proven results). You are much more likely to trust a physician like this over another who does not measure up. If fact, it might be foolish to do otherwise!

How do we judge whether or not a teacher is telling us the truth in class? The professor who can easily establish rapport with students has an advantage (character). We expect the academic credentials to be solid (qualifications). It's also very helpful if he or she is a good communicator, and seems genuinely interested in helping us learn (motive). And, we are more likely to believe our professor if we've had a chance to test his or her material in real life, or we've heard from others that it really works (proven results).

HEAD PROFESSOR

There are many teachers — thousands in the colleges where we train. They rise and fall in prominence, impacting learners to varying degrees. But few of these leaders make contributions that endure beyond their lifetimes. The teachings of one particular professor, however, are diligently sought year after year. Let's listen to some of his positions:

- Happy are the peacemakers, for they shall be called sons of God (Matt. 5:9).

- You have heard that it was said, "You shall love your neighbor, and hate your enemy." But I say to you, love your enemies and pray for those who persecute you (Matt. 5:43–44).

- Do not judge lest you be judged. For in the way you judge, you will be judged; and by your standard of measure, it will be measured to you. And why do you look at the speck that is in your brother's eye, but do not notice the log that is in your own eye? (Matt. 7:1–3).

- Do not lay up for yourselves treasures on earth, where moth and rust destroy, and where thieves break in and steal. But lay up for yourself treasures in heaven, where neither moth nor rust destroys, and where thieves do not break in or steal (Matt. 6:19–20).

- Everyone who hears these words of mine, and acts upon them, may be compared to a wise man, who built his house upon the rock. And the rain descended, and the floods came, and the winds blew, and burst against that house; and yet it did not fall, for it had been founded upon the rock (Matt. 7:25).

GOING TO THE SOURCE

These are the remarkable words of Jesus, words that have been preserved for two thousand years. Profound? Yes! Potentially life changing? Absolutely!

Who recorded these statements? Are the writers trustworthy? At least ten historians who lived in the first century wrote independently about Jesus' life.[1] For example, Josephus, the noted Jewish historian, writing at the end of the first century A.D. records in his book *Antiquities*, 18.3.3:

> Now there was about this time Jesus, a wise man, if it be lawful to call him man, for he was a doer of wonderful works, a teacher of such men as receive the truth with pleasure. He drew over to him many Jews, and also many Greeks. This man was the Christ. And when Pilate had condemned him to the cross, upon his impeachment of the principle man among us, those who had loved him from the first did not forsake him, for he appeared to them alive on the third day, the divine prophets having spoken these and thousands of other wonderful things about him. And even now, the race of Christians, so named from him, has not died out. — Josephus AJ 18.3.3

Many more recent scholars have also worked to document his words and actions. But our most objective and reliable record of Jesus' life was penned separately by four men: Matthew, Mark, Luke, and John.

Their letters, carefully preserved, make up the first four books of the New Testament (the second part of the Bible), and describe the background, birth, travels, teachings, and ministry of Jesus.

Matthew and John were 2 of Jesus' 12 chosen disciples, and traveled with him for three and one-half years. They listened to him speak, witnessed his deeds of kindness, and participated in his ministries. Following Jesus' departure, they spent the rest of their lives proclaiming throughout the Middle East all they had seen and heard. John's testimony concerning Jesus was so powerful that he was exiled by the Roman emperor to a deserted island.

Mark was an assistant of Peter, another of the disciples, and was intimately familiar with the life of Jesus. Mark also traveled extensively with Paul, who became the first to establish churches in the surrounding nations. The fourth author, Luke the physician, also accompanied Paul and Mark in traveling the entire Mediterranean region for the sake of Jesus' message.

All four men were either directly acquainted with Jesus or his disciples. And risking bandits, poverty, arrest, angry mobs, and dangerous sea travel, they all gave their lives to see that people heard his teaching.

How should we use these letters? As history? Entertainment? Fiction? A very important question! Simon Greenleaf, famous Harvard professor of law says:

> All that Christianity asks of men . . . is that they would be consistent with themselves; that they would treat its evidence as they treat the evidence of other things; and they would try and judge its witnesses, as they deal with their fellow men, when testifying to human affairs and actions in human courts.[2]

Let's take Dr. Greenleaf's advice, and look at what these men wrote as we would look at any other documents. Many people have opinions about Jesus' life which are based on little more than speculation. Others claim to have special insight or revelations about what he said. But the most reliable sources by far are the letters written by Matthew, Mark, Luke, and John.

Consider Luke's motive in writing:

> Inasmuch as many have undertaken to compile an account of the things accomplished among us, just as those who from the beginning were eyewitnesses and servants of the word have handed them down to us, it seemed fitting for me as well, having investigated everything carefully from the beginning, to write it out for you in consecutive order, most excellent Theophilus; so that you might know the exact truth about the things you have been taught (Luke 1:1–4).

Luke deeply desired that people know the truth about Jesus. When we read his letter and the other letters today, we can still be assured they are the best possible record of Jesus' life and teachings.

Does Jesus Meet the Tests?

Each of us must also ask, "Is Jesus believable?" We should pose the same questions to him we would pose to anyone else who claims to know the truth. So let the quest begin!

Character. Even a brief look at Jesus' life shows a man of remarkable kindness. He made time for the seemingly most insignificant people. He made friends with the outcasts of His society, like tax collectors and prostitutes (Matt. 9:10–13). Once as Jesus was teaching, some women brought their children for Him to pray over. But the disciples tried to hold them back. Stopping His discussion, Jesus declared, "Let the children alone, and do not hinder them from coming to me; for the kingdom of heaven belongs to such as these" (Matt. 19:14). Then, He gathered the little ones close and prayed over them.

Courage is another of Jesus' hallmarks. Though kind, He also boldly stood for what He knew was true. Entering the temple one day, He found that merchants had transformed it into a market place. Overturning their tables, Jesus cried out, "It is written, 'My house shall be called a house of prayer'; but you are making it a robbers' den" (Mark 11:15–17). When his authority was challenged, Jesus silenced their arguments, and continued right on speaking to the crowds (Matt. 21:23–27).

Jesus is also a compassionate and forgiving person. A woman was caught in adultery, and the religious chiefs brought her to Jesus, demanding the death penalty. Rather than join with them in performing the letter of the law, Jesus defended her life until the very last accuser departed. Then He said quietly to the woman, "I do not condemn you. Go your way. From now on sin no more" (John 8:1–11). Even as Jesus was dying, He prayed aloud for the soldiers who drove nails into His hands and feet, "Father, forgive them; for they do not know what they are doing" (Luke 23:34). Jesus' character is truly radiant among all others.

Qualifications. Most of us would agree that spiritual leaders should possess certain qualities. We would look for a person with a life of prayer and meditation. Jesus is no exception. Frequently, He left the crowds to be alone and to pray (Luke 5:16). Just before choosing His disciples, we read that He prayed for the entire night (Matt. 14:23). His disciples obviously saw the benefits in Jesus' life and wanted the same for themselves:

> And it came about that while he was praying in a certain place, after he had finished, one of his disciples said to him, "Lord, teach us to pray just as John also taught his disciples" (Luke 11:1).

We also expect a leader to promote peace. Jesus lived in a nation under military occupation by the Roman Empire. Some of Jesus' closest friends tried to persuade Him to join the freedom fighters and to even be their leader. But Jesus had a far greater mission. He told his followers:

> Happy are the peacemakers, for they shall be called sons of God. . . . Do not resist him who is evil; but whoever slaps you on the right cheek, turn to him the other also (Matt. 5:9, 39).

As Jesus was being arrested, one of the disciples drew a sword to defend Him. But even in His darkest hour Jesus commanded:

> Put your sword back into its place; for all those who take up the sword shall perish by the sword (Matt. 26:52).

By challenging the impulse of revenge, He was showing His disciples, and all of us, a radically different way to live.

A spiritual leader is also not a person to conceal wisdom, but one who selects and trains followers to be future leaders. While Jesus was often surrounded by a multitude of listeners, He devoted special time to the 12 He had choseN to be His primary messengers (Luke 18:31). As their understanding and faith grew, He sent the men on short journeys to speak to the surrounding villages (Matt. 10:5). In His last instructions to the disciples, Jesus commanded them to do in the lives of others what He had done in their own lives:

> Go therefore and make disciples of all the nations, baptizing them in the name of the Father and the Son and the Holy Spirit, teaching them to observe all that I commanded you (Matt. 28:19–20).

Jesus surpasses every qualification as a spiritual leader.

Motive. A teacher's true motive is a good reflection on the purity of their message. People in our day often become motivated to speak when offered fortune, fame, or freedom. In Jesus' time it was no different, and as a person with a great following, Jesus had access to such rewards. Did He take advantage of them?

The letters of Matthew, Mark, Luke, and John reveal a man who chose to live in poverty. Jesus had no house, no donkey, no money (Matt. 17:24–27). In fact, the only material thing of value we know that Jesus owned were His clothes (Mark 15:24). Not the slightest hint can be found that He was motivated by material wealth. Rather, He taught of the dangers that riches can bring upon people (Matt. 19:23–24).

What about the draw of popularity? People came from all around to hear Jesus speak. The letters document two specific gatherings of both four and five thousand men, in addition to women and children. Jesus' audiences are described as "crowds" 20 times, and as "multitudes" 97 times!

These people longed for hope and leadership. Few of us appreciate what it is like to live under an oppressive government. We assume that our freedoms of speech, travel, and even owning firearms will always be protected. But Israel was under foreign rule. The people yearned for a guide to political freedom. Yet when the people tried to make Jesus their king, He refused (John 6:15). Clearly, becoming a popular political figure was not Jesus' intent. Instead, He kept reminding followers of the deepest meaning of freedom:

If you abide in My word, then you are truly disciples of mine; and you shall know the truth, and the truth shall make you free (John 8:31–32).

Proven results. One of the best tests of any teacher's message is in the reality of day-to-day living. Does it actually work? Many ideas, great as they may initially sound, quickly deflate when taken to the road. How have Jesus' words fared in peoples' lives? Does the world acknowledge the wisdom of His influence? We could refer to any number of facts to the affirmative. Consider these:

- Western law is largely based on the principles found in the Bible, an orientation that has endured in spite of strong philosophies to the contrary.
- Roughly one-quarter of all people in the world today identify themselves as Christians.
- Christian churches are found in the vast majority of the world's many nations.
- More copies of the Bible have been published than any other book. It's been read by more people and published in more languages than any other literary work.

But the best evidence to the strength of Christianity is perhaps not found in the list of accomplishments, but rather in the arena of persecution. The greatest outward challenge to Christianity in our century has been the oppression of communist governments. At the close of World War II, communists took control of China, Russia, Eastern Europe, and much of Africa. With them came rigid enforcement of the humanist/naturalist philosophy, one based on materialism and evolution, and bitterly opposed to any acknowledgment of spirituality. Christians by the tens of thousands were arrested and church buildings were closed or destroyed. In many areas no visible sign of Jesus' followers remained. "We've triumphed over God!" declared many Marxist leaders.

In the late 1980s and 1990s, as communist governments waned in power and fell, we witnessed an inspiring event. Christians from these oppressed nations began to resurface in record numbers — numbers far greater than before Marxism took hold. In spite of official antagonism, trust in Jesus was being passed on, person by person, giving hope in the midst of seeming hopelessness!

People who center their lives on Jesus, in spite of incredible odds, have endured and grown in spite of every trial imaginable. The are perfect witnesses to the durability of Jesus' teachings.

Extraordinary evidence. To top all we've investigated, the life of Jesus was also marked by miraculous events — far beyond that of any other person. The letter of Mark, in particular, highlights the extraordinary and supernatural powers of Jesus. His public teaching began with transforming hundreds of gallons of water into wine at a wedding party (John 2:1–11). He multiplied a few loaves of bread and fed thousands of hungry people who had come to hear him speak (Luke 9:10–17). Jesus was also constantly healing people of physical illnesses in front of many witnesses (Luke 17:11–19; Matt. 12:10–13; John 4:46–54; Mark 7:24–30). What was His motivation to do these things? Matthew gives a picture:

> As Jesus and his disciples were leaving Jericho, a large crowd followed him. Two blind men were sitting by the roadside, and when they heard that Jesus was going by, they shouted, "Lord, Son of David, have mercy on us!" The crowd rebuked them and told them to be quiet, but they shouted all the louder, "Lord, Son of David, have mercy on us!" Jesus stopped and called them. "What do you want me to do for you?" he asked. "Lord," they answered, "we want our sight." Jesus had compassion on them and touched their eyes. Immediately they received their sight and followed him (Matt. 20:29–34).

Clearly, Jesus is concerned for those who are hurting. Yet there is also much more. Jesus' primary intention is that the miracles illustrate the enormous truth that He is God and that His message is incredibly powerful. Consider this example: Some leaders were criticizing Jesus for offering forgiveness to a paralyzed man, when Jesus replied:

> Why are you reasoning in your hearts? Which is easier, to say, "Your sins have been forgiven you," or to say, "Rise and walk?" But in order that you may know that the Son of man has authority on earth to forgive sins," — he said to the paralytic — "I say to you, rise, and take up your stretcher and go home." And at once he rose up before them, and took up what he had been lying on, and went home, glorifying God (Luke 5:22–25; NASB).

The supernatural events of Jesus' life make it imperative that we sit up and listen to what He says. Yet none of the events compares with those of His last days. Jesus claimed that He would prove himself through one final miraculous demonstration — His own physical return to life after death (termed "the Resurrection"). Not only did Jesus foretell how this would take place, but it was also prophesied hundreds of years in advance (Mark 9:9–10; John 2:19–22; Ps. 16:10–11; Isa. 53:10–12).

When Israel's leaders condemned Him to death, Jesus was treated as any other prisoner. Roman soldiers were proficient executioners. The history of their empire is strewn with thousands of crosses on which they crucified their enemies. Nailing Jesus' wrists and ankles to the poles and setting the cross upright, they monitored His slow death by hemorrhage and suffocation as they had done with countless other enemies.

The soldiers oversaw His burial in a cave. Once a boulder was placed over the entrance, more soldiers stood guard. A seal was even embedded on the entrance, declaring by authority of the Roman governor that no one could enter.

But then something awesome happened (Matt. 28:1–11). All four writers describe how an angel appeared, petrifying the guards. He rolled away the stone to show the world that Jesus was not there. He had risen! News spread quickly, both to the disciples, and to the Jewish authorities.

Over the next days, Jesus enjoyed many moments with the women and men who were His followers: walking on a journey together, having breakfast by the sea, eating dinner side by side, and speaking at length to as many as one hundred and fifty at one time (Luke 24:13–35; John 21:10–14; Mark 16:14).

Speaking about the resurrection of Jesus, noted British attorney Sir Edward Clarke writes:

> As a lawyer, I have made a prolonged study of the evidences for the events of the first Easter Day (the day of Jesus' resurrection). To me, the evidence is conclusive, and over and over again in the English High Court I have secured a verdict on evidence not nearly so compelling as this. . . . The Gospel evidence for the resurrection I accept unreservedly as the testimony of truthful men to facts they were able to substantiate.[3]

JUST WHO IS JESUS?

By all evidence, Jesus is the most remarkable person who has ever lived, out-shining every emperor, president, physician, entrepreneur, philanthropist, philosopher, or professor in history. Jesus' resurrection alone is evidence that all He ever said is true.

But who is He really, on the inside? Let's listen to the man speak for himself. Mark records Jesus on trial before the rulers of Israel. The cost for being honest about His identity had never been higher, for blasphemy (the crime of claiming to be God) carried the death penalty:

> Again the high priest asked him, "Are you the Christ, the Son of the Blessed One?" "I am," said Jesus. "And you will see the Son of Man sitting at the right hand of the Mighty One and coming on the clouds of heaven." The high priest tore his clothes. "Why do we need any more witnesses?" he asked. "You have heard the blasphemy. What do you think?" They all condemned him as worthy of death (Mark 14:61–64).

JESUS: THE CREATOR

Jesus is God, the one who created the universe, our world, and all living creatures. With power and intelligence beyond imagination, He conceived the cosmos. Jesus is the one who designed the cells and their DNA, who planned the organ systems, and produced the first of each living thing. John refers to Jesus as the "Word" in this introduction to his letter:

> In the beginning was the Word, and the Word was with God, and the Word was God. He was with God in the beginning. Through him all things were made; without him nothing was made that has been made (John 1:1–3).

Later in the New Testament, Paul describes Jesus' role in creation:

> For by Him all things were created: things in heaven and on earth, visible and invisible, whether thrones or powers or rulers or authorities; all things were created by him and for him. He is before all things, and in him all things hold together (Col. 1:16–17).

Just looking at our world alone can give you and me some insight into the awesome nature of God. When we stand on a mountaintop, gaze at a roaring river, observe animals in nature, or look at night deep into outer space we gain an appreciation of the immenseness of God. Over 100 billion galaxies are out there! We can begin to relate to the feelings experienced by King David when he wrote:

> The heavens declare the glory of God: the skies proclaim the work of his hands (Ps. 19:1).

Learning the fascinating intricacies of biology, the wonderful complexity of genetics, the amazing interactions of human physiology can also bring us to exclaim as David did:

> For you created my inmost being; you knit me together in my mother's womb. I praise you because I am fearfully and wonderfully made; your works are wonderful, I know that full well (Ps. 139:13–14).

Creation is a constant affirmation, a continuous reminder, of God's intelligence, power, and goodness:

> How many are your works, O LORD! In wisdom you made them all; the earth is full of your creatures (Ps. 104:24).

Dr. Robert Jastrow, director of the Goddard Institute for Space Research, insightfully observes:

> Most remarkable of all is the fact that in science, as in the Bible, the world begins with an act of creation. That view has not always been held by scientists. Only as a result of the most recent discoveries can we say with a fair degree of confidence that the world has not existed forever; that it began abruptly, without apparent cause, in a blinking event that defies scientific explanation. Now we see how the astronomical evidence leads to a biblical view of the origin of the world. The details differ but the essential elements in the astronomical evidence and the biblical account of Genesis are the same.
>
> The chain of events leading to man began suddenly and sharply, in a definite amount of time — in a flash of light and energy. The astronomers are so embarrassed by this that for the scientist who has lived by his faith in the power of reason, the

story ends like a bad dream. He has scaled the mountain of igno-rance, he is about to conquer the highest peak when he finds him-self face to face with a group of theologians who have been there for centuries![4]

For the person with open eyes, evidence of God's creative work is ev-erywhere to be found: in astronomy, physics, bioscience, and chemistry. But to see it, we must first open our eyes, both literally and figuratively, and look around.

THE BIBLICAL ACCOUNT OF CREATION

God can do anything. He is all-powerful, timeless, and all-intelligent. It goes with the job description. To some people, the universe may appear old. But God made stars with visibility immediately available to the earth "to declare His glory," in the same way as He made the first apple tree with fully mature apples and the first man and woman mature and grown. God is not ever to be placed into a naturalistic box. He is a superhuman being.

God could have created the universe in any way, over any amount of time He chose. He could have done it all in five nano-seconds if desired. God could have accelerated or decelerated the expanse of the universe, ac-celerated or decelerated the speed at which light travels, or modified the "laws" of nature in any way He might have chosen.

So how did He actually create the universe? Genesis, the first book of the Bible, gives the only eyewitness account — God's account — of the origin of the universe and living organisms. Jesus Christ makes reference to this account:

> From the beginning of creation, God created him [Adam and Eve] male and female (Mark 10:6).

Many people have heard of Genesis, but few have actually read it. So rather than take other people's word for Genesis, let's read the account for ourselves.

• **Day 1** — Genesis 1:1–5

In the beginning God created the heavens and the earth. Now the earth was formless and empty, darkness was over the surface of the deep, and the Spirit of God was hovering over the waters. And God said, "Let there be light," and there was light. God saw that light was good, and he separated the light from the darkness.

God called the light "day," and the darkness he called "night." And there was evening, and there was morning — the first day.

On the very first day we see the origin of the four dimensions: time, energy, space, and matter: "In the beginning (time) God created (energy) the heavens (space) and the earth (matter)." The earth was created as an amorphous mass, and hung in space.

• **Day 2** — Genesis 1:6–8

And God said, "Let there be an expanse between the waters to separate water from water." So God made the expanse and separated the water under the expanse from the water above it. And it was so. God called the expanse "sky." And there was evening, and there was morning — the second day.

On the second day, God gave form to the earth. Atmosphere containing thick water vapor — sometimes called a "canopy" — was separated from the water covering the planet, similar to the one covering Venus today. Later on, this canopy likely produced a greenhouse effect, leading to warm weather all over the earth. The canopy may also have filtered sunlight, and contributed to longer life spans of the first people.

• **Day 3** — Genesis 1:9–13

And God said, "Let the water under the sky be gathered to one place, and let dry ground appear." And it was so. God called the dry ground "land," and the gathered waters he called "seas." And God saw that it was good. Then God said, "Let the land produce vegetation: seed-bearing plants and trees on the land that bear fruit with seed in it, according to their various kinds." And it was so. The land produced vegetation: plants bearing seed according to their kinds and trees bearing fruit with seed in it according to their kinds. And God saw that it was good. And there was evening, and there was morning — the third day.

On day 3 God brought up the continents from the ocean floor and dry land appeared, separating the oceans. God created all mature vegetation, each unique plant species "according to its kind," emphasizing each species' distinction from all others.

• **Day 4** — Genesis 1:14–19

And God said, "Let there be lights in the expanse of the sky to separate the day from the night, and let them serve as signs to mark seasons and days and years, and let them be lights in the expanse of the sky to give light on the earth." And it was so. God made two great lights — the greater light to govern the day and the lesser light to govern the night. He also made the stars. God set them in the expanse of the sky to give light from darkness. And God saw that it was good. And there was evening, and there was morning — the fourth day.

On this day, God created the sun and the moon and the stars, placing them in the space around the earth. Note that the plants created on day 3 were certainly dependent upon the sunlight that appeared the following day.

• **Day 5** — Genesis 1:20–23

And God said, "Let the water teem with living creatures, and let birds fly above the earth across the expanse of the sky." So God created the great creatures of the sea and every living and moving thing with which the water teems, according to their kinds, and every winged bird according to its kind. And God saw that it was good. God blessed them and said, "Be fruitful and increase in number and fill the water in the seas, and let the birds increase on the earth." And there was evening and there was morning — the fifth day.

On the fifth day, God created fish, other water inhabitants, and birds.

• **Day 6** — Genesis 1:26–31

And God said, "Let the land produce living creatures according to their kinds: livestock, creatures that move along the ground, and wild animals, each according to its kind." And it was so. God made the wild animals according to their kinds, the livestock according to their kinds, and all the creatures that move along the ground according to their kinds. And God saw that it was good.

Then God said, "Let us make man in our image, in our likeness, and let them rule over the fish of the sea and the birds of the air, over the livestock, over all the earth, and over all the creatures that move along the ground." So God created man in his image, in the image of God he created him; male and female he created them. . . . God saw all that he had made, and it was very good. And there was evening, and there was morning — the sixth day.

THE SIX DAYS OF CREATION

DAY 1

DAY 2

DAY 3

DAY 4

DAYS 5 AND 6

On this day, God created mammals and other land creatures. God then topped off his design by creating man and woman.

• **Day 7** — Genesis 2:1–3

Thus the heavens and the earth were completed in all their vast array. By the seventh day God had finished the work he had been doing; so on the seventh day he rested from all this work. And God blessed the seventh day and made it holy, because on it he rested from all the work of creating that he had done.

God rested; creation was complete.

In Genesis chapter 1 we find God's brief but profound explanation of the origin of matter, time, energy, space, and all types of life. Note that each kind of life that has ever existed was created, and lived together, during this time. Over the years, we have observed some small variations or adaptations within species, but no sign of transition from one species to another.

Genesis chapter 1 is clearly intended as a chronological or step by step description, similar to observing the assembly of a car at an automobile plant. Chapter 1 is like watching as the car goes through the plant — from the body, to the wheels, the engine, the paint, the interior, and finally to a person driving it away.

In Genesis chapter 2 we next read a short recounting of creation, with an emphasis on the role of humans, and the critical decisions they are about to make. The Genesis 2 viewpoint would be that of an observer recording the driver's cruising down the road and the events leading up to their wreck. More about this in a moment.

WHAT ABOUT "THEISTIC EVOLUTION"?

Trying to find a compromise between evolution and the Bible's account, some leaders teach "theistic evolution," an attempt to sanitize evolution by claiming that both are compatible. Theistic evolution teaches that God was indeed the creator, but did so through the means of evolution.

Some people welcome this approach as a way of conforming both to the scientific community and to their spiritual convictions. There exist, however, numerous problems with the entire concept of theistic evolution:

• Evolution itself is still scientifically unsupportable. The evidence, rather, points toward design and intentional creation by God.

- Evolution's ideas of mutation and survival of the fittest are completely foreign to the concept of God as personal and nurturing.
- Evolution's proposal for the development of life is grossly inconsistent to that documented in the Bible.

One of the main principles of theistic evolution is that the six "days" of creation are really six "ages" or long periods of time — time that would be necessary for evolution to take place. But what does the Bible really say?

Genesis uses the word "*yom*" for "day." Careful analysis of the Bible's use of this word shows that, when combined with a number (such as "first" or "second"), it always refers to a normal-length day; not an age, era, or any other extended period of time. The Genesis "day" was no longer or shorter or different than any other. References to the "morning" and "evening" of these first days (such as in Gen. 1:5, 8, 13, 19, 23, 31) are further evidence to the use of the word in the literal sense.

The Hebrew word *yamim* (plural for *yom*) appears over 700 times in the Old Testament. When used in a historical context (as in Gen. 1) it always refers to literal 24-hour days. For example, when explaining the commandment to observe the Sabbath (the day of rest), Moses makes reference to the literal, 24-hour days of creation:

> For in six days *[yamin]* the LORD made the heavens and the earth, the sea and all that is in them, and rested on the seventh day; therefore the LORD blessed the Sabbath day and made it holy (Exod. 20:11; NASB).

and

> So the sons of Israel shall observe the Sabbath, to celebrate the Sabbath throughout their generations as a perpetual covenant. It is a sign between Me and the sons of Israel forever; for in six days the Lord made heaven and earth, but on the seventh day He ceased from labor, and was refreshed" (Exod. 31:16–17; NASB).

On this subject, Arthur F. Williams explains the findings of many scholars:

> We have failed to find a single example of the use of the word "day" in the entire Scripture where it means other than a period of 24 hours when modified by the use of the numerical adjective.[5]

Interpreting "days" as "long periods of time" also leads to some other interesting inconsistencies. For example, Genesis says that on day 3 God created mature vegetation species, including fruit. If a day was a "long period of time" (hundreds of millions of years) then how did these plants survive without the sun and photosynthesis? The sun was not created until day 4. Plants also require carbon dioxide for their metabolism. Yet animals, the source of carbon dioxide, were not created until day 5. And how did all the flowers pollinate without the insects and birds, also created on day 5?

God can do anything, including creation of life and the universe in an instant, if so desired. If we are going to be consistent with the Bible's record, creation was completed in six, normal-length days, not ages, or any other vast time periods.[6]

The only way to assert that evolution and "religion" are compatible is to regard "religion" as having nothing to do with the real world, and nothing to do with the Bible's record. A God who "created" by evolution is, for all practical purposes, indistinguishable from no God at all.

Michael Denton, in his book *Evolution: A Theory In Crisis*, explains:

> As far as Christianity was concerned, the advent of the theory of evolution and the elimination of traditional theological thinking was catastrophic. The suggestion that life and man are the result of chance is incompatible with the biblical assertion of their being the direct result of intelligent creative activity.
>
> Despite the attempt by liberal theology to disguise the point, the fact is that no biblically derived religion can really be compromised with the fundamental assertion of Darwinian theory. Chance and design are antithetical concepts, and the decline in religious belief can probably be attributed more to the propagation and advocacy by the intellectual and scientific community of the Darwinian version of evolution than to any other single factor.[7]

Evolution and theism (belief in God) are completely incompatible. They are as different as day and night. While trying to please both camps, many people compromise both their science and their faith. The result can only be a watered-down version of the two, and that's no way to live.

How Old Is the Universe?

Genesis explains that the universe and all other living things were created at essentially the same time as were humans. The Bible contains a careful record of each generation. It records Adam (the first created man), Adam's sons, grandsons, great-grandsons, and so forth. The lineage continues through Noah, Abraham, King David, and on to the birth of Jesus. See Genesis 5:1–32, Luke 3:23–38, and Matthew 1:2–16. Even the life span of some people is recorded.

We can estimate the age of the universe by counting the number of generations, and multiplying this by the number of years between each generation. Reasoning like this, and correlation with other historical events, point toward creation occurring approximately 6,000 years B.C. In chapter 3 we discussed scientific methods used for measuring the earth's age, and found the evidence also indicates a young planet. The Bible's record is consistent with that concluded by numerous researchers.

Dr. John Eddy of the High Altitude Observatory in Boulder, Colorado, in an article in the prestigious journal *Geotimes*, declares:

> There is no evidence based solely on solar observations that the sun is 4.5 to 5 billion years old. . . . Given some new and unexpected results to the contrary . . . I suspect that we could live with Bishop Ussher's value for the age of the earth and sun [a few thousand years].[8]

Dr. Harold Slusher, an astrophysicist and geophysicist, conducted exhaustive research and found:

> There are a number of indicators that seem to indicate an age of no more than 10,000 years, at the very most, for the solar system and the earth.[9]

Enormous scientific evidence exists to support the Genesis account. Robert Jastrow describes what more and more astronomers are concluding:

> Now we see how the astronomical evidence leads to a biblical view of the origin of the world. The details differ, but the essential elements in the astronomical and biblical accounts of Genesis are the same: the chain of events leading to man commenced suddenly and sharply at a definite moment in time, in a flash of light and energy.[10]

Genesis does not answer every question regarding the events of creation. It does, however, give us a basic understanding of our origins and a glimpse of the awesome nature of God, enough so we can agree with Paul:

> By faith we understand that the universe was formed at God's command, so that what is seen was not made out of what was visible (Heb. 11:3).

Dr. Arthur Compton, Nobel Prize winner in physics, certainly understood the role of such confidence:

> For myself, faith begins with a realization that a supreme intelligence brought the universe into being and created man. It is not difficult for me to have this faith, for it is incontrovertible that where there is a plan, there is intelligence, an orderly, unfolding universe testifies to the truth of the most majestic statement ever uttered — "in the beginning God."

TRUST THE CREATOR

Naturalists declare that there is no God, only the evolutionary powers of nature at work. The "Star Wars" approach tries to impress on us that God is only an impersonal "force" floating in the cosmos. The "New Age" movement tells us there exist many mystical "gods," and that we ourselves can become one, too.

The truth is that Jesus is the Creator of everything. Jesus is not just "nature;" neither is He some detached "force," nor just one of many gods. More than just the Creator, He is a person, a person who is interested in you and me.

Think of it. The one of incredible super-intelligence and universe-creating power is an individual who is focused and passionate in his affection for each and every person. Just look at what Jesus says:

- I am the light of the world (John 8:12).
- I am the bread of life. He who comes to me shall not hunger, and he who believes in me shall never thirst (John 6:35).
- The thief comes only to steal, and kill, and destroy; I came that they might have life, and might have it abundantly (John 10:10).
- I am the resurrection and the life; he who believes in me shall

live even if he dies, and everyone who lives and believes in me shall never die (John 11:25–26).

- I am the way, the truth, and the life. No one comes to the Father, but through me (John 14:6).

Forget about crediting nature, "using the force," or collecting mystic crystals. Have questions about life? Trust the Creator. Perplexed over personal decisions? Trust the Creator. Dealing with guilt or sorrow? Trust the Creator. Need help with relationships? Trust the Creator.

Jesus is the only one truly worthy of our trust, regardless of what others say, in spite of conflicting feelings within, and regardless of any prior "religious" experience. Jesus offers us the key to what we desire most: lasting inner security, deep happiness, and answers about our universe. He should know. He designed and produced it all!

In spite of this truth, people repeatedly ignore the Creator. Thinking themselves strong enough, smart enough, or just too busy, they push aside Jesus' tenderness and advice. This is what the Bible calls "sin." Basically, sin is trying to somehow live without Jesus in our lives. It's far more than actions like lying, or stealing, or killing. It's also more than just thoughts like jealously, envy, anger, or lust. Essentially, sin is believing that we can find security, happiness, and universal answers outside of the Creator. Paul expressed this clearly:

> For since the creation of the world God's invisible qualities — his eternal power and divine nature — have been clearly seen, being understood from what has been made, so that men are without excuse. For although they know God, they neither glorified him as God nor gave thinks to him, but their thinking became futile and their foolish hearts were darkened. They exchanged the truth of God for a lie, and worshiped and served created things rather than the Creator — who is forever praised. Amen (Rom. 1:20–25).

This is the problem described in Genesis chapter 5. The first man and woman decided to ignore God's advice and tried to find answers their own way. This event was the first of billions to follow, as humankind still tries in vain to live without God, and suffers the terrible consequences. Trusting evolution in spite of its flaws and evidence to the contrary is just one example of the extremes to which people will go to find answers outside of

God. As a result, our culture continues to suffer the gross human devaluation and alienation from God that evolution demands.

David Needham, explains this situation well:

> Sin is the expression of man's struggle with the meaning of his existence while missing life from God. It is all the varieties of ways man deals with and expresses his alienation from his Creator.[11]

DECISION TIME

But we don't have to go on ignoring God. Jesus' mission in coming to earth was to tell us the truth, rebuild our relationship, and to pay the price we owe for ignoring God. All He asks of you and me is that we make a decision to trust Him; that we respond to His love with our hearts, our thoughts and affections. His message is so clear and refreshing:

- I have come into the world as light, so that no one who believes in me should stay in darkness (John 12:46).

- Repent [turn your heart around] and believe the good news (Mark 1:15).

- Yet to all who received him, to those who believed in his name, he gave the right to become children of God (John 1:12).

- For God so loved the world, that he gave his one and only Son, that whoever believes in him shall not perish, but have eternal life (John 3:16).

- I tell you the truth, he who believes has everlasting life (John 6:47).

- I am the resurrection and the life. He who believers in me will live, even though he dies; and whoever lives and believes in me will never die (John 11:25–26).

Information about Jesus is not enough. Facts about Him are insufficient. Rather, a personal decision must be made. Are you trusting Jesus today, trusting Him for security and leadership in your life?

If not, any clear-thinking person would be pressed to begin today to build a relationship with the Creator. Your decision to trust Jesus is a very personal one. It's made foremost in your inner heart. It's also the only decision you'll ever make that counts for all eternity. There indeed may never be a tomorrow to make that decision.

Discover more about Jesus and His message to us by reading the letters of Matthew, Mark, Luke, and John. They are located in the New Testament part of the Bible. Find a church made up of people who also trust Jesus, and tell someone about your decision. Realize that you are now living proof of Jesus' promise that, "You will know the truth, and the truth will set you free" (John 8:32) — free from erroneous ideas, free to receive God's love, free to be deeply happy and fulfilled throughout your life.

Allow yourself to fully appreciate the marvels and awe of all He has made: the stars, our world, and life itself. Be fully thankful for Jesus' passionate love, that God himself desires to be close to you. Take a stand and tell others the truth about the One who created the universe.

Summing Up

Scientific evidence points toward intentional design and creation. But just who is the Creator? Several have made such claims. To gain our confidence, we examine the character, qualifications, motive, results, and extraordinary evidence for each contender. Only Jesus Christ meets the qualifications. He is the Creator.

Genesis chapter 1 contains God's account of creating the universe, the earth, and all living things. While Genesis does not answer every question, it does give us a basic understanding of our origins and a glimpse of the awesome nature of God.

Jesus is not an impersonal force. Rather, He is affectionate toward each person, and wants us to experience His love. You and I must each make a choice. We can go on believing false ideas and missing out on Jesus. Or, we can embrace the truth about creation, life, and the God who passionately wants us to trust Him.

Endnotes

1 Josh McDowell, *Evidence That Demands a Verdict* (Campus Crusade for Christ, 1972), p. 84–89.
2 Simon Greenly, *Testimony of the Evangelists, Examined by the Rules of Evidence Administered in Courts of Justice* (Grand Rapids, MI: Baker Book House, 1965), p. 46.
3 John R.W. Stott, *Basic Christianity* (Downers Grove, IL: Inter-Varsity Press, 1971), p. 47.
4 Robert Jastrow, *God and the Astronomer* (New York, NY: W.W. Norton, 1978).

5 Bert Thompson, *Creation Compromises* (Montgomery, AL: Apologetics Press, Inc., 1995), p. 139, quoting Arthur F. Williams, *Creation Research Annual* (Ann Arbor, Michigan: Creation Research Society, 1965), p.10.

6 Thompson, *Creation Compromises,* p. 139, quoting Henry M. Morris, *Scientific Creationism* (Green Forest, AR: Master Books, Inc., 1974), p. 223–224.

7 Michael Denton, *Evolution: A Theory in Crisis* (London: Burnett Books, 1985), p. 66.

8 Wayne Jackson *Creation, Evolution, and the Age of the Earth* (Stockton, CA: Courier Publications, 1989), p. 5, quoting John Eddy, *Geotimes* (September 1978): p.18.

9 William J.J. Glashouwer and Paul S. Taylor, "The Earth, a Young Planet," a film produced by Eden Communications, Gilbert, AZ, 1983, quoting Harold S. Slusher.

10 Jastrow, *God and the Astronomers*, p. 15.

11 David Needham, *Birthright: Christian, Do You Know Who You Are?* (Portland, OR: Multnomah Press, 1979), p. 25.